Murder Most Vile
Volume 24

18 Truly Shocking
Murder Cases

Robert Keller

**Please Leave Your Review of This Book at
http://bit.ly/kellerbooks**

ISBN: 9781793966018

© 2019 by Robert Keller

robertkellerauthor.com

Table of Contents

Final Deployment

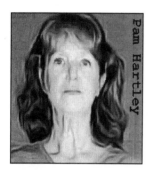

Lt. Lee Hartley was gravely ill, and the medical staff aboard the USS Forrestal did not have a clue as to what was wrong with him. The Forrestal class supercarrier had departed its home base of Mayport, Florida, on June 8, 1982, for a five-month deployment to the Mediterranean. Now, four months later, Lt. Hartley was in such a poor state of health that the decision was taken to airlift him from the ship and fly him back to the military hospital in Jacksonville.

Lieutenant Hartley's symptoms had first appeared about one month into the deployment. At first, he'd reported severe stomach cramps and a strange tingling sensation in his extremities. A stint in the ship's infirmary and treatment for gastroenteritis seemed to stabilize his condition, but a couple of weeks later, the symptoms were back – with a vengeance. Now, the lieutenant was in constant agony, he complained of being cold, sores began to appear on his lips and in his mouth, his complexion began to take on a peculiar gray hue. That was when the decision was made to get him off the ship.

But doctors at the Navy hospital in Jacksonville, with all of their advanced technology, fared no better in diagnosing Hartley's illness. Their best bet was liver disease or hepatitis. And whatever was ailing the lieutenant, his stint in the hospital did not improve his condition. On November 18, 1982, he eventually succumbed to organ failure. Given the agony of the previous five months, death must have been almost a relief.

Lee Hartley's family, especially Pam, his wife of just one year, were devastated by his death. And they were soon to receive shocking news. Doctors had been unable to determine the cause of Lee's ill health, but an autopsy would quickly get to the bottom of it. Hartley's liver, his kidneys and blood contained nearly 1,000 times the natural levels of arsenic.

The Naval Criminal Investigative Service (NCIS) is a law enforcement agency tasked with investigating crimes in the U.S. Navy and Marine Corps. With the revelation that Lt. Hartley had died of poisoning, the agency was ordered to launch an inquiry, with Special Agents Jerry Whitacre and Walter O'Brien assigned to the case. Their initial theory was that Hartley may have come into contact with the poison accidentally. But an audit of the ship's inventory soon put paid to that idea. There was nothing on board that would account for it. And that left only one option. Lt. Hartley had been murdered.

But who among the Forrestal's 5,000 crewmen might have wanted Hartley dead? As it turned out, quite a few. Lt. Hartley had been head of the ship's disciplinary department, so it had been his job to dole out punishments to wayward sailors. That had earned him more than a few enemies among the enlisted men. In fact, Hartley had told his father in a letter that one sailor had come at him with a sword. Strangely, though, he hadn't reported the incident to his superiors.

NCIS, in any case, favored another suspect, the person who stood to gain most from Hartley's death, his grieving widow Pam. The only problem with that theory was that Pam had been thousands of miles away at the time her husband was poisoned. Or had she? Further digging turned up the fact that the Hartleys had rendezvoused in Benidorm, Spain while the Forrestal was docked there and Lee was on shore leave. During that stop, they had hung out with another navy couple and Pam had made breakfast for the group, as well as several cocktails. A few hours later, both Lee and his navy colleague had suffered severe abdominal cramps. The other man soon recovered, but over the weeks that followed, Lee's condition got steadily worse.

The NCIS investigation uncovered other information to support their theory about Pam Hartley. Pam had once been enlisted in the Navy but now worked as an environmental technician with the Department of Energy. In that capacity, she had access to various poisons, including arsenic. The Hartleys' marriage was also not as blissful as it appeared on the surface. Lee Hartley was a jealous man and Pam a flirtatious woman. This toxic combination had led to a number of spats at the Naval Officers' Club, which had not gone unnoticed.

Delving deeper, NCIS agents learned that Lee had been married before. But his apparently happy, 16-year marriage had come to an end after Pam had been assigned to his office as a clerk. The two had soon become involved in a torrid affair with Lee eventually divorcing his wife and marrying Pam. Inquiries at the Officers' Wives' Club turned up more interesting revelations. It appeared that Pam could be quite forthcoming after a few drinks. She'd told more than one woman that she found it difficult to remain faithful while Lee was away at sea. And on one occasion, she'd made a flippant comment about hiring a hitman to get rid of him.

Under questioning, Pam said that she could not recall making the remark and insisted that she loved Lee and would never do anything to hurt him. Asked to take a polygraph, she immediately agreed. The investigative team was certain that the test would back up their suspicions, but the results threw them a curve ball. Pam Hartley passed with flying colors.

And then there was another setback to the investigation. The toxicology report was in, and it revealed something startling. An analysis of Lee's hair follicles allowed pathologists to determine the pattern of his arsenic ingestion. It showed that Lee's first exposure to the toxin had come weeks before he'd hooked up with Pam in Benidorm and had continued at regular intervals long after Pam had returned to the States. That seemed to get Pam off the hook and sent investigators back to the formidable task of assessing the 5,000 suspects aboard the Forrestal.

But who among them had both motive and opportunity? Could it possibly be Lee Hartley's cabin mate, Lt. Samuel Yates? The two men had an apparently good relationship. Then again, they were rivals for promotion to Lieutenant Commander. And Yates may have had another motive. It appeared that he had begun spending time with the grieving widow soon after Lee's death. Some reports even suggested that he'd seduced her at the funeral.

So was Yates their man? The early signs said…maybe. Blood tests on Yates showed elevated levels of arsenic, consistent with having handled the poison. But there might have been another explanation. Yates had been Hartley's cabin mate over several months and thus would have been exposed to the same environmental factors as the dead man. He might have ingested the poison this way. In any case, Yates was soon ruled out as a suspect. Tests carried out on his belongings showed no trace of arsenic. Had he handled the poison, those traces would almost certainly have been transferred to the other objects he'd touched.

All of the main suspects had now been eliminated, forcing investigators to consider some bizarre theories. One was that Hartley had committed suicide by purposely dosing himself with arsenic. That idea was quickly discounted after a psychologist analyzed Hartley's recent letters and said that he found no suggestion of suicidal thoughts. The ingestion of small amounts of poison over an extended period also did not fit with the typical pattern of suicide. Why subject yourself to months of agony when there are faster, less painful methods?

A more plausible theory was that Hartley had taken the arsenic not to kill himself but rather to make himself ill. According to his family, he had recently spoken about being fed up with long deployments and wanted to be assigned to a desk job back in Florida. Perhaps he'd taken the poison to get himself off the ship and back to shore where he could be with his wife. If that was the case, then Hartley could not have chosen a worse toxin. Once taken, arsenic is not expelled from the body. Instead it accumulates in cells and tissue, and its effect becomes multiplied over time.

This theory, like the others, would ultimately be discarded. If Hartley had handled arsenic, there should have been traces of it on his possessions. Nothing was found. Aside from that, Hartley had continued to ingest the poison even after he was airlifted from the Forrestal. If his intention had been to get off the ship, why wouldn't he have stopped taking the poison once that goal was achieved? The simple answer was that he would. One year into the investigation and with no more leads to pursue, the case went cold. It would remain so until 1995.

That was the year that NCIS formed a cold case unit. One of the first cases it was assigned was the unsolved murder of Lee Hartley. However, the investigative team soon hit a major roadblock. In the intervening 13 years, all of the physical evidence had been destroyed. All that was left were medical records and the written reports of the original investigative team.

Undeterred by this setback, the agents set about re-interviewing as many of the original witnesses as possible. Soon a pattern emerged. Almost everyone they spoke to seemed to think that Pam was somehow involved. There was no real evidence, of course, but the young woman's behavior, during the time that Lee was in the hospital, had definitely raised eyebrows. While her husband lay dying, Pam could often be found hanging out in the parking lot, joking and horsing around with hospital staff. The investigators got another disconcerting piece of intel. Pam's brother, Ron, revealed that she had once approached him with an offer of cash in exchange for killing Lee. It was time to interview the widow Hartley.

Pam had benefited handsomely from her husband's death, receiving a $35,000 insurance payout, $10,000 a year in veterans' benefits, and free military medical care for life. But the interceding years had not been good to her. After blowing through the insurance money, she'd lapsed into a cycle of alcohol and drug abuse. Currently she was receiving treatment for addiction at a hospital on a military base. It was there that investigators tracked her down.

Under interrogation, Pam soon broke down. According to her, her marriage to Lee Hartley had not been a happy one. Lee was extremely possessive and stifled her in everything she wanted to do. Within a year, she had grown to despise him. Despite this, she was not about to walk away. She loved the status attached to being a Naval officer's wife and was not prepared to give that up. And if she couldn't be a Navy wife, then the next best thing was to be a Navy widow. By the time Lt. Hartley departed on his final deployment aboard the USS Forrestal, his wife had decided to kill him.

The way that she went about it was ingenious. Pam knew that Lee had a sweet tooth, and so she started to send him care packages of home-baked cookies and his favorite, whiskey cake. All of these treats were generously laced with arsenic, a colorless, odorless poison. She firmly believed that he would be dead within weeks.

But to her surprise, Lee didn't die, not even when she upped the dosage. It was time for a new plan. When Lee had shore leave in Benidorm, she flew to Spain to spend time with him. There, she dosed his food and drink with arsenic, accidentally poisoning his navy buddy in the process. Even after Lee was airlifted to the hospital in Jacksonville, she continued her campaign, feeding him poisoned apple juice as he lay in his bed. That, as it turned out, was the fatal dose. Lee Hartley died the next day.

Pamela Hartley would ultimately be charged with second-degree murder, pleading guilty. When asked at her trial why she had murdered her husband, she offered the quite ludicrous explanation that she wanted to end their marriage but didn't want to hurt his feelings by divorcing him. Hartley was sentenced to 40 years in prison. She was paroled in 2012, having served just 16 years behind bars.

Jigsaw Man

During the Spring of 2009, police in Hertfordshire, England were presented with a baffling and particularly gruesome puzzle to solve. It started on the morning of Sunday, March 22, when a truck driver stopped for a breather along the A507 highway near Cottered and spotted a green gym bag sitting on the tarmac. The man went to unzip the bag and instantly wished he hadn't. Inside, wrapped in plastic and secured with duct tape, was a human leg.

Seven days later, on March 29, a pedestrian in Wheathampstead discovered another bag, this one containing a human forearm, cleanly severed at the wrist and elbow. And there was an even more macabre discovery on March 31. A farmer crossing a field in Asfordby, Leicestershire found a severed human head, with its eyes, ears, tongue and facial skin removed.

By now, the police had opened a murder docket and had formed a task force (named Abnet) to discover the identity of the victim and to track down the killer. Initial progress was not encouraging. DNA matching proved that all of the body parts were from the same person but revealed nothing about that person's identity. The teeth were a promising lead but, thus far, the police had not been able to match them to any individual. Neither had the missing persons database been of any help. All that the police knew for sure was that the victim was male. That had been established by a team of forensic anthropologists, using the shape and dimensions of the skull as their reference.

On April 7, with the task team no closer to the identity of the victim, a driver on the A10 discovered another gym bag, this one containing the victim's other leg. That was followed four days later by the discovery of the torso, found in a ditch near Standon, Hertfordshire. Now, at least, investigators were able to pin down the cause of death. The victim had suffered a single stab wound to the back, delivered by a blade approximately four inches long. The thrust had penetrated a lung and, while it had ultimately been fatal, it would not have been a quick death. According to pathologists, the victim would have taken at least an hour to die.

But who had delivered that fatal wound? And who was the victim? Desperate for answers, the police decided to go public with an appeal for information. Soon, every major newspaper in the country was carrying front page stories about the case, and the mystery corpse had acquired a media nickname. He had been dubbed "Jigsaw Man."

Before long the Operation Abnet incident room was being flooded with calls, each of them claiming to know Jigsaw Man's identity. One of those, in particular, caught the attention of task force investigators. On April 21, a woman phoned in to report that she had been unable to contact her son, Jeffrey Howe, for over a month. Jeffrey, she said, traveled frequently for work but always made a point of keeping in touch with her. She'd heard nothing from him since early March. Since this tallied with the time frame of the murder and since Howe matched the physical description and age of Jigsaw Man, the police decided to look into it.

Jeffrey Howe was a 49-year-old businessman from Southgate, London. Trained as a chef, he currently ran his own business, selling kitchen equipment to restaurants and hotels. Single and with no family other than his mother, Howe was known to be gregarious and outgoing. Although some residents at his Southgate apartment complex said that he could be confrontational, it appeared that he was generally well liked. Several of those interviewed said that he had a heart of gold and would help anyone in need.

And it appeared that Howe had recently shown his charitable side by taking in a down-on-his-luck friend. When officers knocked on the door of Howe's apartment it was opened by 20-year-old Sarah Bush. According to Bush, she was living there with her boyfriend, 38-year-old Stephen Marshall, a friend of the owner. Questioned by investigators, Marshall said that Howe had taken him and Bush in when they had no place to stay. They'd been living in the apartment, rent-free, for over five months. When investigators asked about Howe's whereabouts, the couple said that they hadn't seen him in over a month.

But the story just did not sit right with the detectives, especially as the couple appeared jumpy and could not explain why they hadn't reported Howe missing. A search of the apartment was then carried out, finding nothing but nonetheless rousing suspicion. The place had recently been given a thorough cleaning, and the officers wondered whether that had been intended to get rid of forensic evidence. At this point, it was decided to take both Marshall and Bush into custody.

In the UK, suspects in a serious crime can be held in custody for 72 hours before they must either be charged or released. This placed tremendous pressure on the investigative team. They were convinced that Marshall and Bush were involved in Jeffrey Howe's murder. Now they had just three days to gather evidence before the suspects walked free. A forensics team was, therefore, dispatched immediately to the apartment.

In the meantime, detectives started questioning Marshall and Bush, walking into a dead end as every question they asked was met with a terse "no comment." They had better luck when looking into the backgrounds of the suspects. They both had criminal records – Bush for prostitution and Marshall for a long list of crimes, including assault, drug dealing, and weapons offences. He'd also been the main suspect in a savage murder in which a man had been stabbed to death and then burned in an apparent attempt to destroy evidence. No charges had been brought in that case, due to lack of evidence.

While this was ongoing, Jeffrey Howe's apartment was turning up a wealth of evidence. Despite the considerable effort that had been put into the clean-up, there were areas that had been missed. Under a carpet in the bedroom, crime scene technicians found a large bloodstain. They also found blood spatter in the bathroom and another patch of blood under a bath mat. The implication appeared to be that Howe had been attacked in the bedroom, possibly while he was sleeping, and then dragged into the bathroom and dismembered there.

But that still didn't prove that Marshall and Bush were the killers. In order to link them to the murder and dismemberment of the body, forensics experts had to rely on fiber evidence. Several fibers had been found clinging to the duct tape that had been used to secure the body parts. Now those fibers were determined to have come from three sources – Jeffrey Howe's mattress, an air mattress that Marshall and Bush had been sleeping on, and a green t-shirt belonging to Marshall.

Marshall and Bush were arraigned for murder on May 1, 2009, with both entering "not guilty" pleas. That meant that the matter was definitely going to trial, and while prosecutors were confident in their forensic evidence, there was one thing that they had yet to establish – motive. Why had Marshall and Bush suddenly decided to kill their benefactor? Why kill the man who was allowing them to live rent-free in his home? Had there been some kind of altercation? Had Howe grown tired of their freeloading and asked them to move out? Had he made improper advances towards Sarah Bush?

The police did not have the answers to those questions, but what they did have was Jeffrey Howe's financial records. These showed that Marshall and Howe had funded a spending free on Howe's credit cards after his death. They showed also that Marshall had deposited forged checks from Howe's bank account into his own. He'd also pawned Howe's cellphone and had gone so far as to open an eBay account in Howe's name and then sell Howe's Saab motor vehicle via the site. The motive for murder thus appeared to be financial. Jeffrey Howe had been murdered so that his killers could plunder his cash and assets.

Stephen Marshall and Sarah Bush went on trial at St Albans Crown Court on January 12, 2010. But before the jury had even been sworn in, Marshall indicated that he wanted to speak to prosecutors. He now admitted to cutting up Howe's body and disposing of it. However, he denied murder, saying that it had been Bush who'd killed Howe.

Confronted with these allegations, Bush told an inverted version of Marshall's story. She admitted to helping dispose of the body but said that Marshall was the killer. This scenario, where co-accused try to lay the blame on each other, is commonly called the "cutthroat defense." But it made little difference to the prosecution, they proceeded with murder charges against both defendants.

And the evidence against the pair was pretty conclusive. Aside from the forensics and circumstantial evidence, there was CCTV footage of Marshall and Bush driving towards Leicestershire the day before Jeffrey Howe's head was found in a field there. There were also witnesses who testified that Marshall had bragged to them about his prowess in getting rid of bodies. A friend of Sarah Bush told the court that Bush had boasted about killing Howe, saying that she had held a pillow over Howe's face to stop him screaming after Howe had stabbed him.

Faced with the overwhelming evidence against them, Marshall and Bush decided to change their pleas to guilty on February 1, three weeks into the trial. He now pleaded guilty to murder, she to perverting the course of justice. The jigsaw had finally been solved.

Stephen Marshall was sentenced to life in prison and must serve a minimum of 36 years before he is eligible for parole. Sarah Bush got off far more lightly. Her sentence was just two-and-a-half years, and she was released after fourteen months.

FOOTNOTE: While serving his prison sentence, Stephen Marshall has admitted to the dismemberment and disposal of four more bodies which he claimed to have hacked apart with knives, a hatchet, and a chainsaw. According to him, he did this while he was in the employ of an infamous London crime family. He'd put that expertise to use in disposing of the man who had once called him friend.

For I Have Killed

John Feit

To the red-blooded young men of McAllen, Texas, Irene Garza was an unattainable dream. Irene had grown up among them, attending McAllen High School and going on to Pan American College where she had graduated with a teaching degree. In between times, her movie star good looks had won her a spate of beauty pageants, including the 1958 Miss All South Texas Sweetheart. With her sparkling brown eyes, porcelain skin, lush brunette hair and waiflike figure, it was easy to see why the judges had chosen to place the crown on her head. It was also easy to see why she turned heads wherever she went.

Yet for all her loveliness, Irene was a shy young woman, a devout Catholic who was a member of the Legion of Mary and attended Mass and Communion every day, without fail. Rumor had it that this religious devotion was the reason behind her recent break-up with Sonny Martinez, one of only two men who Irene had ever dated seriously. Whether that was true or not, Irene was now 25 years old and single, a state of affairs that did not seem to bother her overtly.

Her twin passions in life were her religion and her career as a second-grade teacher.

On the evening of Saturday, April 16, 1960, Irene told her parents that she was going to confession at her regular parish, Sacred Heart Church in McAllen. A number of parishioners saw her at the church that night and saw her enter the confessional, only to emerge a short while later with Father John Feit. The two of them then walked together towards the church rectory. Although this was unusual, no one paid particular attention. It was not unheard of for congregants to visit the vicarage.

Neither did Irene's parents concern themselves too much when their daughter had not yet returned home by the time they retired to bed. Irene often stayed after confession to attend midnight mass. However, when Nicholas Garza got up for a drink of water in the middle of the night and peered into his daughter's bedroom, he was alarmed. Irene wasn't there and there was no indication that her bed had been slept in. At 3:00 a.m. that Sunday morning, Nicholas called the McAllen police and reported his daughter missing.

Tracing the steps of the missing woman, detectives soon learned that she had last been seen at Sacred Heart Church. Father Feit confirmed that she'd been there and said that he'd taken her confession. It appeared that he'd been the last person to see her. After that, Irene had simply vanished, leading the police to conclude that she'd run off, perhaps with a lover. That theory did not go down well with the Garzas who insisted that their daughter would never have done such a thing. Everyone who knew Irene, agreed. Someone had taken her, they said, and not with any good purpose in mind. That assessment would turn out to be tragically accurate.

On Monday, April 18, after what was the biggest missing person search in the history of Hidalgo County to that point, searchers found Irene Garza's purse on a remote road just outside of town. A few yards further on lay her left shoe. Caught on a fence nearby, a lace veil fluttered in the breeze. All of this suggested that Irene had met with foul play.

There was hope the following day when a woman phoned the Garza residence and claimed, over a crackly connection, to be Irene. She said that she had been kidnapped and was being held at a hotel in nearby Hidalgo. That call, unfortunately, turned out to be a sick hoax. The real Irene Gaza was found three days later, on April 21, floating face down in a canal, several miles away from where her purse and shoe had been found. Josephina Garza collapsed to her knees on being told of her daughter's death, emitting a long, dreadful moan that those present later described as "like the howl of a wolf."

The mystery of Irene Garza's whereabouts had been resolved. Now it was up to the police to find her killer. But they faced a formidable challenge from the outset. The body had been in the water for nearly five days, and that had ensured that trace evidence like blood, hair, and semen had been washed away. The medical examiner was, however, able to establish cause of death, as well as the probable motive for the murder. Severe bruising to both eyes and to the right side of her face suggested that Irene had been savagely beaten. The theory was that she had been unconscious when her killer raped her. Then, after sating his lust, he'd pulled a cord around the unfortunate woman's throat and strangled her to death.

But who would have done such a thing to the beautiful and popular teacher? The police didn't know yet, but they were determined to find out. Over 500 interviews were conducted, taking McAllen detectives as far afield as San Antonio. Fifty individuals, including Sonny Martinez and Irene's other former boyfriend, were subjected to polygraphs. In addition, the authorities put up a $2,500 reward for information, and local businessmen swelled that reward by an additional $10,000. It all led nowhere other than to a possibility that no one seemed prepared to countenance – that Irene Garza had been raped and murdered by her parish priest, 27-year-old Father John Feit.

The evidence, though, didn't lie. Father Feit was the last person to see Irene alive; he was seen walking with her towards the rectory; parishioners told police that his confession line had moved particularly slowly that night and that he was away from the sanctuary several times; fellow priests reported that they had noticed scratches on his hands at midnight mass. All of this pointed the finger of suspicion at the padre, but the most damning piece of evidence was yet to come. A few days after the discovery of Irene's body, the police drained the canal and discovered a photo slide projector lying in the mud at the bottom. This was traced by its serial number and found to have been recently bought by Father Feit. So what was it doing there? Was it possible that the heavy object had been used in an attempt to sink the body to the depths? Perhaps Father Feit had an answer.

But if the police thought that the priest would crack when faced with such incriminating evidence, they were wrong. Feit sat calmly smoking a cigarette as he informed the investigators that he had no idea how his projector had ended up at the bottom of the canal. Perhaps the killer had stolen it at the same time that he'd abducted Irene. Feit had ready answers to all the other questions put to him as well. After initially denying that he had taken Irene to the rectory, he admitted that he had gone there with her, but only because she had asked to give her confession "in private." Quizzed about his absences from the confession box, he said that he had broken his glasses and had gone home to fetch a replacement pair. On arrival, he'd found that he'd left his keys back at the church and had therefore had to climb the rough brick to a second floor window. That was how he got the scratches on his hands. Feit was then asked to take a lie detector test and agreed. The following day, the McAllen Police Department announced that he had passed his polygraph and was no longer considered a suspect.

But should Feit have been so easily eliminated from the investigation? His history suggests not. Just three weeks before Irene Garza's death, a woman named Maria Guerra had been raped while praying at another Catholic church in the area. Father Feit, who had been visiting the church on the day of the attack, was mentioned as a possible suspect, but local church leaders stepped in to quash the stories. Despite their efforts, Feit was later charged, although his trial resulted in a hung jury. The matter was due before the courts again in 1962, but Feit circumvented that by agreeing to plead no contest to a reduced charge of aggravated assault. He was ordered to pay a fine of $500.

After the conclusion of the Guerra case, Feit was sent by the church to Assumption Abbey, a Trappist monastery in Missouri. There, he was counseled by a monk named Dale Tacheny who was told to evaluate Feit and decide whether he had the disposition to join the friary. Apparently, Tacheny decided that Feit did not have the correct temperament to become a monk because Feit ended up at a treatment center for troubled priests in Jemez Springs, New Mexico. He later became a member of staff at the center and remained there until he quit the priesthood in the 1970s. Thereafter, he got married, fathered three children and settled in Phoenix, Arizona, where he remained active in church affairs. For 17 years, he was a volunteer at a food charity run by the Society of Saint Vincent de Paul.

The murder of Irene Garza, meanwhile, had long been confined to the cold case files with little chance of a resolution. That was until 2002 when Dale Tacheny contacted the police in San Antonio and told them that he could no longer keep what Feit had told him a secret. According to Tacheny, Feit had confessed to him that he had raped and murdered Irene Garza.

Texas Ranger Rudy Jaramillo was given the task of re-examining the Garza evidence. That led him to Father Joseph O'Brien, a colleague of Feit's at the time of the murder. O'Brien had always denied knowing anything about Irene Garza's death, but under pressure from Jaramillo, he eventually admitted that Feit had confessed to him shortly after the murder. Jaramillo next interviewed the polygraph examiner who had tested Feit back in 1960 and found to his surprise that Feit had not passed the test. According to the examiner, the decision to say that Feit had passed had come "from above." He suspected that local authorities might have been placed under pressure by the Catholic diocese.

Jaramillo had conducted just two interviews and had already uncovered enough evidence to bring the matter before a grand jury. Unfortunately, for the Garza family, still desperate for justice, Hidalgo County D.A. Rene Guerra disagreed. He called O'Brien senile and suggested that Jaramillo had acted inappropriately in conducting his interviews. When the matter did eventually come before the grand jury, Guerra's performance was shoddy, at best. He failed to obtain subpoenas from Tacheny and O'Brien and declined to call the polygraph examiner as a witness. As a result, the grand jury decided that there were insufficient grounds for an indictment against Feit. Guerra then compounded the anger of the Garza family by making an incredibly insensitive statement to the media: "Why would anyone be haunted by her death? She died. Her killer got away."

But Guerra would pay a political price for his uncaring attitude. In 2014, district court judge Ricardo Rodriguez campaigned against him, with the Garza case a key issue. Rodriguez won by a landslide and was good to his word. In April 2015, he announced that the Garza case was open again. In February 2016, former priest John Feit was arrested in Scottsdale, Arizona. A month later, Feit was extradited to Texas to stand trial.

Feit was 83 years old by now and in poor health, suffering from stage 3 kidney and bladder cancer. Nonetheless, there is no statute of limitation on murder. Hauled before a Hidalgo County court in late November 2017, Feit entered a not guilty plea. The evidence, however, said different. Father O'Brien had died in the intervening years, but there was still the deposition given by Dale Tacheny. There was also the evidence from the original investigation, all of which pointed to Feit as a cold-blooded killer.

On December 7, 2017, the jury returned a guilty verdict against John Feit. The following day, the same jury rejected pleas from his defense attorney, asking for probation on account of his advanced age and poor health. Feit was sentenced to life in prison. Justice had taken its time, but after 57 years, the killer of Irene Garza was behind bars at last.

Madman at the Mall

Wade Frankum

About seven miles west of Sydney's central business district lies the suburb of Strathfield, a peaceful, family-oriented enclave that is also one of the most multi-cultural in Australia's largest city. It is a place of wide avenues and natural vegetation, of country-style estates, Victorian terraces and high-rise apartments. A good place to live, in other words, offering the best of urban and suburban living. It is hardly the kind of place where you'd expect one of Australia's worst ever crimes to occur. And yet that is exactly what happened on the afternoon of Saturday, August 17, 1991, a day when evil came calling in Strathfield.

Fifteen-year-old Roberta Armstrong had come to the Strathfield Plaza shopping mall that afternoon to meet up with a friend at a popular coffee shop, the Coffee Pot Café. A student of the nearby McDonald College, Roberta was a popular and gifted girl who excelled academically, was a talented ballerina and also played the flute in the school band.

Seated at the table next to Roberta and her friend was a strange man. Dressed in jeans, a denim jacket and a grey beanie and with a large cardboard tube sitting on the table in front of him, the man appeared agitated, his eyes darting from one patron to the next. His main focus, though, seemed to be the young girls sitting at the next table. They, however, paid him no mind, even when he got up from his chair and reached into his jacket. Then, without warning, he drew a large knife and plunged it into Roberta's back, withdrew and plunged it in again, repeating the action four times as pandemonium broke out in the restaurant.

Roberta Armstrong never stood a chance. The weapon was a 20-inch Bowie knife with a finely honed blade. It sliced through skin and sinew, skewering vital organs and blood vessels on its path. But even as the gravely-injured teenager slumped forward with the knife still embedded in her flesh, the killer was reaching for the cardboard tube on the table before him. These cylinders are typically used to hold posters, blueprints or other large documents. This one, however, had been employed to conceal a semi-automatic rifle. Now that weapon was in the killer's hands, and that was when the shooting started.

Sixty-one-year-old Joyce Nixon, seated at a nearby table, was killed in the initial salvo. So too was her 36-year-old daughter, Patricia Rowe, who put herself between the gunman's bullets and her two young children. Then café owner George Mavris emerged from the kitchen and walked straight into a hail of gunfire. The gunman then shifted his line of fire, cutting down Carol Dickinson, 47, her daughter Belinda, 20, and Belinda's 17-year-old friend, Rachelle Milburn.

With people now cowering behind tables and pot plants in the café, the shooter moved away, heading casually in the direction of Franklin's Supermarket, firing as he walked. Helen Xu was hit in the arm and another woman suffered wounds to her legs before the gunman got Robertson Kan Hock Voon in his sights and fired off a burst, cutting down the 53-year-old where he stood. The shooter then took the stairs to the upper level carpark where he fired at a young couple, Beulah Patrick and Brett Lenane, injuring both. Mall employee George Sidawy was shot in the leg, hand, stomach, and arm but survived. Bullets also raked across a vehicle driven by Margaret Lampe but fortunately missed her. Not so lucky was Gregory Read who had bravely run ahead of the shooter, warning people to take cover. He ended up being shot in both feet for his courage.

With police units now racing towards the scene and most of his targets cowering behind cars, the shooter shifted focus, standing at the edge of the rooftop and directing fire towards the adjacent Strathfield Railway Station and taxi rank, injuring two passers-by. Then Catherine Noyes made the grave mistake of trying to escape the rooftop in her car and found the gunman blocking her path, his rifle pointed directly as her. The man then forced his way into the vehicle and ordered her to drive him to Enfield.

Catherine Noyes obeyed the instruction, of course, even though she was almost too petrified to operate the vehicle's controls. But the terrified woman had covered barely a dozen yards when the killer did the last thing she would have expected. He suddenly burst out crying. "I'm sorry, I'm so sorry" he wept. "Please stop." Then with the wail of approaching sirens becoming ever more strident, he scrambled from the car, put the rifle barrel under his chin and pulled the trigger.

The siege of Strathfield Plaza was over but those fifteen minutes of mayhem had extracted a heavy cost. Eight people, including the gunman, lay dead. Six had been injured and countless more would bear emotional scars for a very long time. As emergency responders transferred the injured to local hospitals, carried the dead to the morgue and comforted the traumatized, as police officers cordoned off the area and began gathering evidence, questions were already being asked. Who was the shooter and what had possessed him to do such a terrible thing?

The first part of that question was easy. He was Wade Frankum, a 33-year-old taxi driver from North Strathfield. The second part was far more difficult. Frankum had never been in trouble with the law, had no history of violence and had never been diagnosed with mental illness. Why then had he suddenly decided to murder seven strangers? As is often true of these cases, the answer may lie in his childhood.

Born to an alcoholic, manic-depressive mother and a submissive, uninvolved father, Wade had had big expectations placed upon him from childhood. From his earliest school days, he would be locked into a room alone with instructions to study. The expectation was that he would excel academically, but the pressure placed on him was immense. Even 99 percent was considered inadequate with his mother demanding to know "what happened to the other 1 percent." Counter-balancing that was the assertion that he was better than other children and that was why so much was expected of him. There was very little affection, only demands and admonishments.

Given these conditions, it is hardly surprising that the boy grew up with deep feelings of inadequacy. Being set unrealizable goals will do that to a child. Eventually, he burned out, and his academic performance fell off. He graduated school but with mediocre results. Thereafter, he drifted from one dead end job to another, eventually ending up as a part-time taxi driver. To a man like Wade Frankum, who had been pressured since childhood to do better than his peers, his life must have seemed like a massive failure. And it was about to get worse.

In 1985, Frankum's father died of emphysema. Five years later, in April 1990, his mother took her own life by gassing herself in her car. Frankum, who had taken his father's death in his stride, was devastated by his mother's suicide. Not even the $30,000 inheritance he received from her estate could cushion the blow. He was soon blowing through that money in any case, spending almost all of it on prostitutes.

And perhaps the idea of a shooting spree was already beginning to ferment in his brain. In September 1990, he obtained a gun license and in January 1991, he bought a 7.62mm SKS self-loading assault rifle. In April, he purchased the 20-inch Bowie knife that he would later use to such horrific effect against Roberta Armstrong. All the while, Frankum was seeing a psychiatrist for depression and spending his nights seeking out prostitutes or watching pornography. He also developed an obsession with the Brett Easton Ellis novel, "American Psycho," the disturbing story of a wealthy businessman who becomes a serial killer.

According to Dr. Rod Milton, a forensic psychiatrist who was brought in to develop a profile of the killer in the aftermath of the shootings, Frankum's plans began to gather momentum after he ran out of money to pay for prostitutes. The sex had served as a "release valve" for him. Without it, the frustrations he harbored about his life began building. The pressure continued to grow until that Saturday afternoon when he walked into the Strathfield shopping mall carrying a gun.

But this was no spur of the moment thing. Frankum had definitely planned it beforehand. In the days leading up to the massacre, he'd had his Bowie knife sharpened and had bought 100 rounds of ammunition for his rifle; the day before, he'd had his hair cropped into a military style cut; on arriving at Strathfield rail station that morning, he'd advised a station porter (who he knew) to "go home."

The Strathfield Massacre did, at least, have one positive outcome. In its aftermath, there was a massive public outcry, putting pressure on politicians to bring in stricter gun control laws. Still, it would take five years and an even greater tragedy at Port Arthur before automatic weapons were finally banned in Australia.

Shots Fired

Piper Rountree

In the early morning hours of October 30, 2004, 911 operators in Richmond, Virginia, were suddenly inundated with a flurry of calls from the city's quiet Tuckahoe Village neighborhood. Each of the callers reported the same thing – they had heard shots fired. One also added that he had seen someone running from the home of Professor Fredric Jablin at 1515 Hearthglow Lane.

Officers were immediately dispatched to the area and found a peaceful suburban street where nothing appeared to be amiss. That was until they called at the Jablin residence and found the professor lying in a pool of blood in his driveway. The 52-year-old academic was still in his pajamas and slippers. It appeared that he'd been shot as he stepped outside to pick up his morning newspaper. The question was: who would have wanted to do such a thing?

Professor Jablin's neighbors were as baffled as the police. They described him as a lovely man who was devoted to his three children, to his job, and to his students at the University of Richmond's Jepson School. No one had a bad thing to say about him, but a bit of digging soon presented investigators with a likely suspect. Fred Jablin had recently come through a contentious divorce during which he'd gained sole custody of his children, aged 8, 12, and 15. His former wife, Piper Rountree, had been none too happy about that nor about the financial settlement, which she'd described as "grossly unfair." That gave her a solid motive for murder. People have killed for far less reason.

Looking into Rountree's background, detectives discovered that she was no lightweight. She was the daughter of a medical surgeon who had carved a career for herself as an attorney and had once served as a prosecutor in Texas. Piper had met Fred Jablin in 1981, when she was studying at the University of Texas at Austin and he was a lecturer there. Recently divorced, Jablin had been attracted to his pretty student and she to him. However, they had kept their relationship on a strictly professional level until after she graduated. Thereafter, they became romantically involved and more or less inseparable. In 1983, they'd moved to San Antonio, Texas, after Piper was accepted as a law student at St. Mary's University. The move meant a 180-mile commute for Jablin, but he appeared happy to make the sacrifice so that he could spend more time with his gorgeous, young girlfriend. The couple married later that year while Piper was still enrolled in law school.

To those who knew Fred and Piper, the marriage appeared to be a "match made in heaven." Below the surface, though, cracks had begun to appear. Piper was at the time seeing a counselor for "emotional problems related to family issues." She had also been diagnosed with bulimia.

And things would only get worse once Piper graduated and the family moved back to Austin. There was a listlessness about her, a dissatisfaction with her life. In quick succession, she gained and lost a series of plum jobs, including that as assistant district attorney for Hays County, Texas. She then worked for a private law firm and as an attorney for the Texas Classroom Teachers Association. None of those positions lasted longer than two years as Piper either quit of was fired for poor performance. Eventually, she set up her own practice, although she gave it up within a year because Fred was offered a new position with a significant salary increase at the University of Richmond. They could certainly do with the extra money. Piper's uneven work record and her habit of overspending put a strain on the family's finances, especially as they by now had two young children, Jocelyn and Paxton. A third child, Callyn, would follow a couple of years after they settled in Virginia.

After Callyn's birth, Piper put her career on hold so that she could devote herself to her young children. But as with every other job she'd had, she soon tired of being a full-time mom. Her dissatisfaction was exacerbated by serious bouts of depression and by an ectopic pregnancy that resulted in her having to undergo a hysterectomy. Floundering, she turned outward for attention and started an affair with a married ophthalmologist. The doctor would soon regret his indiscretion as Piper began stalking him and making death threats against his wife. When Fred heard of the affair, he was devastated. Deciding that there was no way to save the marriage, he asked Piper to move out of the family home. In March 2001, he filed for divorce.

Piper, as can be expected, did not respond well to this turn of events. She suffered an emotional breakdown and began drinking heavily and abusing prescription drugs. She also began telling anyone who would listen that it was she who had instituted the divorce on account of

Fred's physical and emotional abuse. No one really believed her, and the truth would finally be told when the matter came to court. Then evidence would be presented that documented Piper's unstable emotional state, her substance abuse, her affair. There was also testimony about how she had ruined the family's finances with her reckless spending, running up debts of over $50,000 on one credit card alone. Given her obvious inability to function as a responsible adult, it was no surprise when the judge granted the divorce and gave sole custody of the children to Fred. Piper was also ordered to pay $890 a month in child support while Fred got the bulk of the couple's assets. The outcome left Piper fuming.

Piper was, of course, given visitation rights, but in March 2002, she moved back to Texas. She hoped to practice law again, but the legal office she set up in Houston failed and, within a year, she was clerking for a land title company. In August 2003, she filed for bankruptcy and moved in with her sister. Six months later, she was found in contempt of court in Virginia for failing to pay child support.

By September 2004, Piper owed her former husband over $10,000 in arrear alimony payments. Given her financial problems, it was unlikely that she would ever have made that up. In any case, she told friends, she had no intention of paying Fred the money since she hardly ever saw her kids. Then, in October 2004, her financial obligation was deftly removed when Fred was gunned down outside his home.

Piper was immediately a suspect in Fred Jablin's death. But, as she defiantly told detectives, she could not have done it since she was "halfway across the country" at the time. The police, of course, were

not about to take her word on that. They began looking into her
movements around the time of her ex-husband's murder. It did not
take long before cracks began to appear in her story.

The first evidence against Piper Rountree emerged when police
checked her cell phone records and found that she'd been in Virginia
on the day of Fred's death. Investigators then began checking with the
airlines to see if she'd been booked on any flights from Texas to
Virginia around that time. She hadn't, but there had been a "Tina
Rountree" booked on a Southwest Airlines flight at 4:30 p.m. on
October 28. That flight had taken off from Houston's William P.
Hobby Airport bound for Norfolk International in Virginia. Tina
Rountree was Piper's sister, and the two bore a strong resemblance to
one another. When police showed a picture of Piper to airport staff and
cabin crew, several said that they recognized her but that she'd had
blonde hair. Further investigation revealed that "Tina" had checked a
.38 revolver for her flight to Virginia. Fred Jablin had been shot with a
.38.

With evidence now that Piper had lied about her whereabouts at the
time of the murder, the police next obtained a search warrant for her
sister's Houston home where Piper was still staying. Their case was
considerably strengthened when they scanned Piper's computer and
found an e-mail order for a blonde wig placed by Piper on October 21.
When they found the wig itself, Piper Roundtree was in deep trouble.

But Piper still had one card to play. She insisted that there was
someone who could confirm that she had been in Texas on the day that
Fred was shot. The man's name was Kevin O' Keefe, and, according
to Piper, she'd had a drink with him at the Under the Volcano bar in

Houston on the evening of October 29. If this alibi were to be substantiated, then the police case would all but fall apart.

Unfortunately for Piper, O'Keefe was not very helpful to her cause. He did remember having a drink with her but couldn't recall the exact day. Also, according to him, Piper had asked him to cover for her. She'd told him that her former boyfriend had been stabbed and that she was likely to be a suspect unless she could come up with an alibi. When O'Keefe agreed, Piper asked him to wait at the bar a while. She then left only to return a short while later with a man who she claimed was a notary. The man asked O'Keefe to sign a statement to the effect that he'd been with Piper on the night of the 29th, but O'Keefe refused. He'd said that the police could call him if they had any questions.

Back in Virginia, the case against Rountree was gaining ever more momentum as investigators tracked down a rental car employee and a hotel clerk who were both prepared to testify that they had dealt with Piper Rountree (using the name and driver's license of her sister, Tina) on the day before Professor Jablin's murder. Since the hotel in question was just five miles from the Jablin residence, it put Piper right in the frame. On November 8, 2004, the police moved in to arrest her.

Piper Rountree was extradited to Virginia where she faced a legal case that, although circumstantial, was overwhelmingly against her. There was the cell phone data, the purchase of the wig, the gun, the Southwest flight, her lies about all of the above, and airline, car rental, and hotel staff who could identify her. There was also her misguided attempt to establish an alibi for herself. Why would an innocent person be so desperate to establish an alibi?

And yet, Piper was adamant that she was innocent and would maintain that stance throughout the trial, even as the evidence stacked up against her. Those denials did her no good in the end. The jury deliberated for only a few hours before returning a guilty verdict and a sentencing recommendation of life in prison. That recommendation was ratified by the judge at the sentencing hearing in May 2003, with the addition of three years for the felonious use of a firearm.

Piper Rountree is currently imprisoned at Fluvanna Correctional Center for Women in Troy, Virginia, where she will remain until at least 2020, when she becomes eligible for parole.

Copycat Jack

William Waddell

The year was 1888 and a killer was running amok on the streets of
London. Already three women were dead, their bodies so horribly
mutilated that there were rumors the killings were not the work of a
man but of some mythical beast. The worst of it was that the killer,
who would later enter the public consciousness as Jack the Ripper,
seemed unstoppable. He would almost certainly kill again. It was just a
matter of when.

To the inhabitants of Birtley, a tiny mining village in County Durham,
the ghastly London murders were a source of macabre fascination.
Like everyone else in the country, they obsessively followed every
gory detail in the papers, discussed them at work, at the dinner table, in
the pub. And yet they were far removed from the drama. The foggy
back alleys of east London might have been on another planet. It bore
no resemblance to their little hamlet. Nothing like that could ever
happen here. Except that it did.

At around 7:20 on the morning of Sunday, September 23, 1888, a man named John Fish was on his way to work, a journey that would take him along the railway tracks to the north of Birtley. Approaching a stretch of rail running in the direction of the Vale Pit colliery, he spotted something in a ditch alongside the tracks. Closer inspection revealed that it was the body of a young woman, lying on her side in a pool of congealed blood. She was quite obviously dead, and so Fish wasted no time. He ran to a nearby house for help and was directed from there to the home of a local police constable, John Dodds. Dodds then accompanied Fish back to the spot and found the woman exactly as Fish had described. He recognized her immediately as a local girl named Jane Beadmore.

A quick inspection of the corpse revealed that Jane had met with a horrible death. There were knife wounds to the face and neck, the second of which would probably have proved fatal. But it was the deep gash to the abdomen that really alerted the policeman's attention. The gut had been crudely ripped open, spilling the victim's intestines from the wound. To the small town constable, who had followed the Whitechapel murders with a keen interest, that presented a harrowing proposition. Had the Ripper come to Birtley?

Apparently, this was a serious consideration among the investigating officers. So serious, in fact, that they contacted London's Metropolitan Police and requested assistance. As a result, Inspector Thomas Roots and Dr. George Bagster Phillips were dispatched to the Northeast. Phillips was the Divisional Surgeon for Whitechapel and had performed the postmortem on the latest Whitechapel victim. He would go on to become one of the leading Ripper experts. One look at Jane Beadmore, though, and he was willing to proclaim that this was not the work of the Whitechapel fiend. Common consensus was that the Ripper was a medical man or, at least, someone with a knowledge of human anatomy. The mutilations performed on this victim's body were crude, described by Dr. Phillips as a "clumsy piece of butchery."

That did not exactly come as a surprise to the local officers. By then they had already zeroed in on a rather more mundane suspect, Jane Beadmore's estranged boyfriend. At 22 years of age, William Waddell was five years younger than Jane. He was known as a somewhat morose young man, quite the opposite to Jane who was always cheery and friendly. Nonetheless, the pair were often seen together and were openly affectionate to one another. There were even rumors that William had proposed, although Jane had recently quashed those when she'd told a friend, Isabella McGuinness, that she wanted nothing more to do with Waddell and had "found someone nicer."

Jane hadn't named this new suitor, but it did not take a genius to figure out that the breakup gave Waddell motive. The police were keen to question him about his whereabouts at the time of Jane's death, but when they went to his lodgings, they found that he wasn't there. He had also not showed up at his job on a local farm where he worked as a laborer. That left the police with one of two possibilities to consider. Either Waddell had killed Jane and fled the jurisdiction, or he'd been killed during the same attack and his body lay somewhere, undiscovered. Most were willing to bet that it was the former.

As a bulletin was sent out to the surrounding towns, asking officers to be on the lookout for a man matching Waddell's description, the police began retracing Jane's steps on the day she died. The young woman had recently been diagnosed with a heart condition and had called on her doctor that day to pick up some medicine. Later, she'd stopped at a local store to buy some toffees, which she said were to offset the bitter taste of the medication. Still later, she'd visited a friend named Dorothy Newall. According to Dorothy, Waddell had showed up during that visit and had sat around looking glum. She'd also noticed that he had been drinking. Jane had been friendly towards him and had even offered him one of her toffees which he'd refused. Eventually, he'd muttered something and stalked off, leaving Jane to continue her visit.

The last sighting of Jane Beadmore was around eight o'clock, after she left the Newall farm. That was when two local men spotted her walking briskly along the road. According to them, she'd been alone. That sighting was close to the spot where she would meet her horrific end.

The police also picked up on another interesting snippet of information. According to William Waddell's landlady, he'd recently acquired a knife in a trade with another lodger. Questioned by police, Thomas Fallon confirmed that he'd done the trade with Waddell. The knife, he said, had a three-inch blade, more than adequate to have inflicted the cuts on Jane Beadmore. Several people had seen the sullen Waddell toying with the knife on the day Jane was killed. They also said that he had been drinking, which they found unusual since Waddell was usually a teetotaler.

All of this was circumstantial, of course. Waddell had a knife, he was upset over his breakup with Jane, he'd been drinking, he'd been in her company earlier that day. Had this been the only evidence presented at trial, Waddell would very likely have been acquitted.

But his flight from the jurisdiction was a bad miscalculation, and so, too, were his attempts to hide his identity from those he encountered during that flight. After leaving Birtley, Waddell had traveled north, heading for Scotland. He'd been spotted at various locations along the Scottish border where he'd approached several farmers, looking for work, giving his name as William Laws. He even duped a police constable into believing his identity. Eventually, though, a sharp-eyed civilian in the town of Yeltholm, two miles across the border with Scotland, pointed him out to PC John Thompson, and Waddell was arrested. The date was October 1, 1888, and William Waddell had been on the run for precisely one week. Now he was on his way back to England to face the justice that awaited him.

News of Waddell's capture had spread like wildfire through the district, and every rail station along the route was crammed with people, all eager to get a look at the "Ripper of the North." When Waddell and his police escort eventually arrived in Gateshead, officers had to form a cordon to ensure that he could be safely moved to the carriage that awaited. He was then taken to the police station, where he was formally charged with the murder of Jane Beadmore. That same afternoon, he appeared at the Gateshead County Police Court and was remanded in custody. Again, a huge crowd was gathered, and the magistrate decided to bar the public from the courtroom. Feelings were running high. There were genuine fears that the mob would tear Waddell apart if they got their hands on him.

But William Waddell was hardly the fearsome killer they imagined him to be. He was a nervous wreck on the point of breakdown, trembling so badly that his legs would not support him. He had virtually to be carried in the dock and stood, all aquiver, with downcast eyes throughout the proceedings. Despite what he was accused of, it was difficult not to feel some sympathy.

The trial of William Waddell began at the Durham Autumn Assizes in Chester-le-Street on Thursday November 29, 1888. Waddell, on the advice of counsel, pleaded not guilty. In truth, the case against him was not very strong. The prosecution had been unable to place Waddell with Jane at the time of her death, they didn't have a murder weapon, and the "suspicious" flecks found on Waddell's trousers might have been pig's blood (the prosecution expert was forced to admit on the stand that he couldn't be sure).

But there was one damning piece of evidence. While being held at the Chester-le-Street Police, Waddell had spoken to a police officer, P.C. Thomas Sykes, about his case. During the course of that conversation, Waddell had apparently told Sykes, "I think I must have been out of my mind as I would not strike at a woman, much less do a thing like this."

That, at least, was how Sykes recalled the conversation, and defense counsel decided not to put Waddell on the stand to counter it. In fact, the defense called no witnesses at all, choosing instead to attack the prosecution case in its summation, calling it weak and circumstantial. The jury, however, disagreed, taking just thirty minutes to return a guilty verdict. William Waddell was then sentenced to hang.

The execution was set for Wednesday, December 19, at Durham Jail. Before it could be carried out, Waddell contacted the prison authorities and said that he wished to confess to the crime. Interestingly, Waddell did not offer the motive that most thought was behind the murder. It was commonly believed that he'd killed Jane over their failed relationship, but Waddell denied this. Instead, he claimed that he had read so many stories about the Whitechapel murders that his mind had become deranged and he'd been compelled to commit a copycat killing. If that is true, then Jane Beadmore might be considered, by extension, to be another victim of Jack the Ripper.

Life is Precious

Lukah Chang

Amy Jane Brandhagen had a regular routine as she went about her work at the Travelodge in Pendleton, Oregon. The 19-year-old housekeeper would walk along the corridor on the upper floor, opening doors as she went, leaving the rooms to air out. She'd then start her cleaning at the last room in the row and work her way back. It was an effective little system and one that Amy Jane had been using since she'd started working at the motel. But on the afternoon of Tuesday, August 14, 2012, her efficiency would work against her. Someone was watching from the public library across the road, studying her every move. As she entered the last room on her roster, he quickly crossed the street, climbed the stairs to the second floor and entered Room 231. Then he waited, lurking in the dark, a knife clenched in his hand.

The intruder struck as Amy Jane entered the bathroom and reached for the light switch. Caught entirely by surprise, the young woman had no chance of defending herself. Still, she fought. Even as the blade was repeatedly plunged into her chest, she clawed at her attacker, burying her nails in his neck, raking away furrows of skin. That only served to spur the killer on. Again and again, he buried the knife in the helpless young woman's flesh. Eventually, the mortally wounded Amy Jane collapsed to the bathroom floor. She wasn't dead yet, but she'd soon lose consciousness as her blood puddled around her. The killer then washed his hands, walked calmly from the room, and left the motel. He'd always wanted to know what it felt like to kill somebody. Now he did.

About two hours later, another maid entered Room 231. Noticing that the bathroom light was on, she headed in that direction and walked in on a scene of utter carnage. Amy Jane's brutalized body lay sprawled on the floor, a puddle of half-congealed blood spreading out around her, blood spattered on every surface in the room. The maid turned and sprinted for the manager's office. Minutes later, the manager was dialing 911.

Pendleton, Oregon, is a small town of some 16,000 residents. Violent crime is rare here, and the first responders had certainly never seen anything like this. The victim lay on her back on the hard tile. She had been stabbed multiple times in the chest (the Medical Examiner would later count eight wounds, most of which would have been fatal). There were also indications that her killer had tried to throttle her. The question was why? Since the young woman still had her cellphone and was wearing a watch and other items of jewelry, this wasn't a robbery. And it wasn't a sex crime either. No attempt had been made to sexually molest the victim. So why had she been killed? Detectives were baffled as to why someone would commit such a high risk crime, in a busy motel in broad daylight, with no apparent motive.

But at least there was one solid clue, the skin trapped under Amy Jane Brandhagen's nails. That was sent for processing, and a DNA profile was extracted. Hopes were high that a match would be obtained from the FBI's CODIS database, but in the end, that search came up empty. As vicious as this crime was, it had apparently been committed by a man with no criminal record.

Initially, the police were convinced that the killer was someone who knew the victim, a jilted ex-boyfriend perhaps. One man, in particular, attracted their interest. The word on social media was that a man named Chancy Yates was involved. Some posters even named Yates outright as Amy Jane's killer. Yates was brought in for questioning and almost begged the officers to take a sample of his DNA so that he could be cleared of the murder. And he was. The DNA didn't match. When the other chief suspect, another of Amy's exes named Jim Sullivan, was also cleared, the investigation was at a standstill. It would remain so for almost a year.

On the evening of Friday, August 9, 2013, a 53-year-old Pendleton resident named Karen Lang went for her after-work jog and failed to return home. After spending several hours searching for her along her usual route, her husband called the police and reported her missing. A search was then organized, continuing through the night until 6:55 the following morning, when Karen was found in the undergrowth of Trailhead Park, near the Umatilla River levee. She had been savagely attacked, her skull caved in by several vicious blows to the head.

Karen was rushed to a nearby hospital, barely breathing and tenuously clinging to life. She had lost a considerable amount of blood, and medical staff were not optimistic that she would survive, putting her chances at one in 100. Yet, somehow, the brave woman did cling on, did survive, and would eventually make a full recovery. She remembered nothing of her ordeal, though, dashing hopes that she might be able to identify her attacker.

Fortunately, the investigators had an even more valuable piece of evidence – CCTV footage from a surveillance camera in Trailhead Park. At 6:17 p.m. on the tape, they picked up Karen entering the park, followed a short while later by a man dressed in khaki shorts and a dark t-shirt. The man follows Karen over a footbridge. In his hand, police can clearly see what looks like a length of pipe. Karen and the man disappear from view until 7:29 p.m., when the man is seen entering a park bathroom, remaining there for around two minutes and then exiting.

The police could not identify the man from the tape, but they knew now the sort of weapon he had used to attack Karen Lang. They knew also that he had left it behind in the park, since he had not been carrying it when he'd entered the bathroom. A concerted effort was therefore launched to find the weapon and, within two hours, delivered results when an officer found the bloodstained pipe close to where Karen Lang had been assaulted. It was sent to the crime lab where technicians were able to lift skin cells from the grip. Then came a stunning revelation. DNA from the pipe matched that taken from under the fingernails of murder victim Amy Jane Brandhagen.

With the revelation that Pendleton had a serial offender on its streets, someone who was very likely to strike again if he wasn't caught, the investigation gained new impetus. The first step taken by the investigative team was to circulate the surveillance pictures to local law officers to see if anyone recognized the man. One of them did. He said that the individual was a young homeless man named Danny Wu. Wu had been arrested a number of times over the past year, usually for vagrancy or other minor charges. He had always submitted meekly to the arresting officers and had never offered resistance.

Checking through Wu's arrest records, detectives noticed that he had a distinctive tattoo on his left wrist, the words "Semper Fi." This Latin phrase mean "always faithful" and is, of course, the motto of the US Marine Corps. Was the man they were hunting a former Marine? Apparently not, if the records were anything to go by. The Corps could find no enlisted man by that name.

With the military angle seemingly closed to them, the Pendleton police decided to put out an APB on Danny Wu. Notices went out to police departments across Oregon and its surrounding states while Wu's face was suddenly staring down from wanted posters and appearing on the evening news. With such extensive coverage, it seemed impossible for him to escape detection, and yet a week went by without a single sighting of the fugitive.

Then, on August 28, 2013, two women were having lunch in the cafeteria of the Pendleton Convention Center when they noticed a strange man lurking in the area. The man was walking between the tables, picking up scraps of food that had been left behind by other diners. He looked vaguely familiar, and one of the women soon realized why that was. He was the elusive Danny Wu. The woman immediately dialed 911, bringing police units to the area. Wu was arrested as he tried to escape into an air conditioning duct. A search would later prove that he had been living in the duct for over a week.

Once in custody, Wu proved to be one of the most co-operative
suspects that Pendleton police officers had ever encountered. First he
cleared up a mystery. His real name was Lukah Chang, and he was
indeed a Marine, although currently AWOL from Camp Pendleton in
California. He made no pretense at innocence when asked about his
involvement in the attacks on Amy Jane Brandhagen and Karen Lang.
Asked why he had murdered Amy Jane, Chang's response was
chilling. "To see how it felt," he replied. When the officer asked how it
had felt, Chang responded that it had been both "empowering and
saddening." Asked to elaborate, he said. "Empowering because I took
a life. Saddening because I realize that life is precious."

Chang later went on to tell his interrogators that he felt no remorse
over killing Amy Jane because "All men are dead. They just don't
know it yet." This stunning statement was delivered in typically
deadpan fashion which only deepened the mystery of how Chang had
ended up this way. His background certainly offered no hint of the
cold-hearted killer he would become.

Lukah Chang had been raised in a strict but loving home by parents
who were both Christian missionaries. Receiving much of his
education via home schooling, he had grown up to be an extremely
introverted boy which made his decision to join the Marines a
perplexing one to his family. The Corps, however, had been good for
Chang. It had brought him out of his shell. He'd even met a young
woman and gotten married. But then a fellow Marine, with whom
Chang had formed a strong bond, had been killed, and it had all started
to unravel. Within weeks, Chang had deserted his wife and gone
AWOL. He'd arrived in Pendleton, Oregon, on August 7, 2012. A
week later, he had murdered Amy Jane Brandhagen.

There can be little doubt that Lukah Chang would have committed more murders had he not been caught. At least now he was off the streets and seemingly willing to accept responsibility for his actions. At his trial, he entered guilty pleas to all of the charges against him and accepted a term of 25 years to life on the murder rap plus 10 years for the attempted murder of Karen Lange. That means that Chang could be free before he turns 50. Hopefully by then he will have accepted the veracity of his own words, that life is precious and should never be willfully taken.

Handsome Devil

Joran van der Sloot was born into a life of affluence and privilege. Entering the world on August 6, 1987, in Arnhem, The Netherlands, Joran was the son of a prominent lawyer and an art teacher. He grew to be a tall, handsome and athletic boy with a talent for soccer and tennis. He also excelled academically and was an honors student in his senior year of high school. But already there were signs of trouble ahead. Joran was the personification of a spoilt rich kid. He was demanding and petulant, lied easily, and seldom, if ever, apologized for his actions. His parents found it almost impossible to control him. In truth, they barely tried. It was far easier to indulge his every whim.

When Joran was 16, his father was appointed as a judge in the Dutch territory of Aruba, off the coast of Venezuela, and the family relocated there. Joran was registered as a student at the International School of Aruba but, although he continued to do well and expressed an interest in attending college in Florida, his life was now dominated by other pursuits. He'd already developed an obsession with gambling and soon had a $5,000 line of credit at a local casino, countersigned by his father. Aside from that, he spent his time drinking and chasing women. Aruba is a popular holiday destination, and Joran, tall and good-looking, with a smooth line of talk delivered in an exotic accent, had a long list of conquests. Not all of these were consensual, apparently. There were rumors doing the rounds that he regularly drugged and raped his dates.

Natalee Holloway was just 18 years old on May 30, 2005, the night she met Joran van der Sloot at a casino in Oranjestad, Aruba. The teenager had recently graduated from Mountain Brook High School in Birmingham, Alabama, and had come on a Caribbean vacation with her graduating class of nearly 100 students to celebrate. After striking up a conversation with the handsome Dutch teen, Natalee suggested that he join her and her friends later at Carlos & Charlie's, a popular local bar. Joran agreed. He then called two friends, brothers Deepak and Satish Kalpoe, and asked if they wanted to meet him at the bar.

By the time the three men arrived at Carlos & Charlie's, the party was already in full swing. Joran soon hooked up with Natalee, and the two of them spent most of the evening together, dancing and drinking heavily. When the party finally broke up, Joran asked a heavily inebriated Natalee if she wanted a ride with him and his friends. Over the protests of her classmates, she agreed and left with the three men. It was the last her friends saw of her.

When Natalee didn't arrive for breakfast the next morning, one of her friends went to check on her and found her room empty and her bed unslept in. The alarm was then raised, resulting in an island-wide search for the teen. Van der Sloot and the Kalpoe brothers were, of course, questioned but they all told the same story – that they'd driven to a beach with Natalee, spent some time there, and then driven her back to her hotel. That was soon proven to be a lie when detectives checked surveillance footage from the hotel and did not pick up the Kalpoe brothers' car on it. Still, it took the police a week to arrest van der Sloot and the Kalpoes. Joran, after all, was connected. His father was one of only four judges on the island and a personal friend of the police chief.

Once in custody, Deepak and Satish Kalpoe changed their story. They now said that they had left van der Sloot and Natalee at a fisherman's hut on a nearby beach. Natalee had insisted on it, they said. Joran, however, contradicted this version of events. He said that the Kalpoe brothers had left him and Natalee on the beach and that he'd had consensual sex with her there. Afterwards, he had wanted to take her back to her hotel but Natalee had refused, saying she wanted to stay on the beach to watch the sunrise. Van der Sloot had left her there and hadn't seen her since.

Unfortunately for van der Sloot, his story did not hold up to scrutiny. The police checked his cell phone and found text messages that linked him to Natalee's death. Also implicated was Paul van der Sloot, Joran's father. Despite his connections, the esteemed judge found himself under arrest. He stood accused of advising his son to dispose of Natalee's body, since the police would not be able to build a case without it. That suggests that there was evidence, at the very least, of a conspiracy. The charges, however, would be dropped, setting father and son free. By the end of the summer, the van der Sloots had packed up and returned to Holland, leaving Natalee Holloway's grieving family none the wiser as to what had happened to her.

Back in Arnhem, Joran van der Sloot enrolled at university to study engineering. However, he seemed unable to let the Holloway case go. In April 2007, he teamed up with journalist Zvezdana Vukojevic to write a book on the case. His intention, he said, was to be "open and honest" about what had happened. More than likely, he was just cashing in on his notoriety. In any case, it backfired badly when the Aruban authorities announced that they were reopening the case based on new evidence. This was believed to relate to a post in an Internet chatroom where van der Sloot had stated that Natalee had died on the night she went missing. Van der Sloot was duly arrested and sent back to Aruba for trial. But again the matter didn't make it into the courtroom. Judges decreed that the new evidence did not warrant a prosecution.

Having had such a narrow escape, one would think that van der Sloot would have guarded against injudicious statements in the future. Not so. In 2008, he was caught in a sting run by Dutch journalist Peter de Vries. De Vries had hired a man named Patrick van der Eem to pose as a drug dealer and to befriend van der Sloot. Van der Eem had then recorded van der Sloot making an admission about Natalee Holloway's death.

According to van der Sloot, he'd had sex with Natalee on the beach. Afterwards, they had gone for a walk during which Natalee, heavily intoxicated, had suffered a seizure. She had died in his arms and there had been nothing he could do to save her. Van der Sloot had then panicked. Certain that he'd be accused of murder, he had decided to get rid of the body. He had then called a friend who owned a fishing boat. The two of them had taken the body out to sea and dumped it in the ocean.

Much to Joran van der Sloot's surprise, his taped "confession" was soon splashed across the media, pushing the case back into the spotlight and sparking calls for a new investigation. But despite public pressure from Holland and from Natalee's family in the United States, the Aruban authorities stood firm. The tape added nothing new to the case, they said. Van der Sloot could have been lying to appear tough to his new friend who he thought was a drug dealer.

Once again, van der Sloot had escaped justice. But this latest furor had made him persona non grata in The Netherlands, and so he decided to seek out fresh pastures. He decamped to Thailand, ostensibly to study at Rangsit University in Bangkok. However, he dropped out after just one semester and bought a sandwich shop near the campus. That, as it turned out, was just a cover for his real business. In November 2008, he was caught on camera negotiating with sex traffickers for the sale of Thai women. Van der Sloot is seen demanding $13,000 for each of the women who he had apparently lured with promises of modeling work in Europe. He fled the country just ahead of the authorities.

In February 2010, van der Sloot's father, Paul, dropped dead from a heart attack while playing tennis. Although the van der Sloot fortune had been severely depleted by legal expenses over the years, there was still enough of an inheritance to fund a comfortable life for Joran. He was also still receiving royalties from his book about the Holloway case. Apparently that wasn't enough. In May 2010, van der Sloot hit on a despicable money-making scheme. He contacted Natalee Holloway's family and offered to reveal the location of her body in exchange for $250,000. After accepting a $15,000 down payment, he directed the family's lawyer to a newly-built housing estate in Aruba where, according to him, Natalee was buried. That turned out to be a lie. Soon after, van der Sloot dropped out of sight again, taking his ill-gotten gains with him.

Van der Sloot showed up next in Peru, where he planned to take part in a poker tournament. He had never lost his obsession with gambling and had participated in events in Thailand, in Macau, and in various other locations. But he was a mediocre player at best. In his most successful year, he netted $12,000, hardly enough to fund the playboy lifestyle he craved. Often, he ended with losses. Now, with $15,000 burning a hole in his pocket, he was certain that he would win big.

On May 30, 2010, five years to the day since Natalee Holloway's disappearance, van der Sloot picked up 21-year-old Stephany Flores Ramirez from a casino in Lima, Peru. The following day, hotel staff arrived to clean van der Sloot's room and found Stephany wrapped in a blood-soaked sheet on the bed. The young woman had been savagely beaten, and an autopsy would later reveal that her neck had been broken. As for van der Sloot, he was nowhere to be found.

Van der Sloot was arrested several days later in Santiago, Chile. He was returned to Peru where he immediately confessed to killing Stephany Flores. He said that he had left her in his hotel room while he went to get coffee and had returned to find her at his laptop computer. When he demanded to know what she was doing, she told him that she was looking for evidence that would tie him to the Holloway murder. Enraged, he had attacked her, barely aware of what had happened until she was lying dead at his feet. He'd acted on instinct, he said, and hadn't been in control of his actions. He did, however, admit to stealing money from Stephany's purse before fleeing.

Van der Sloot would later recant his confession, although it did him no good. Found guilty of murder, he was sentenced to 28 years behind bars. He is currently held at Challapalca Prison in the Peruvian Andes where he has twice been the victim of knife attacks. Once he completes his sentence, he will be extradited to the United States where he faces extortion charges relating to the money he obtained from Natalee Holloway's family under false pretenses.

The Final Cut

Hollie Gazzard was petite and beautiful with a mop of auburn hair and a smile that lit up any room she entered. She was a fashionista, who took great care over her grooming and appearance. With her good looks and fashion sense, she might easily have been aloof and conceited, but instead Hollie was a friendly soul, bubbly and outgoing, with a positive outlook on life. Her dream had always been to work as a hairdresser and, at age 20, she was already the star stylist at a salon in her home town of Gloucester, England. Hollie may have been the new kid on the block, but she was the one who customers asked for by name.

If there was one thing missing in Hollie's life, it was a steady relationship. It wasn't that there hadn't been suitors, just that she hadn't found the right one. At least, that is, until January 2013, when she was introduced to 22-year-old Asher Maslin. Asher was tall and ruggedly handsome with the build of a professional athlete. At 6-foot-1, he towered over the tiny Hollie. He also had a sense of danger about him that Hollie found alluring. That wasn't just perception either.

Asher earned his crust as a bouncer at local night clubs and had a reputation as a "bad boy." Still, there was attraction, and it was mutual. Before long, Hollie and Asher were a couple. Soon, Hollie had arranged for him to meet her family.

But Hollie's mom, Mandy, was less than happy with her daughter's choice in men. Mandy worked at a local school where Maslin had once been a student. She knew him as a troublemaker, a delinquent, someone who had seemed to pride himself on back chatting and disrespecting teachers. Had he changed since then? Mandy could only hope so. She desperately wanted her daughter to be happy, and so she and her husband, Nick, decided to give Maslin the benefit of the doubt.

And, at first, their trust appeared to be vindicated. Maslin was attentive to Hollie, polite and respectful to her parents and to her sister Chloe. He had a good sense of humor and appeared to be a fun-loving individual. Most importantly, Hollie appeared happy in the relationship, which was all that really mattered to her family.

All too soon, though, cracks began to appear in the façade. Maslin started to become increasingly controlling of Hollie, demanding to know her every move and plaguing her with constant phone calls and text messages. He also began to become verbally abusive towards her, often in public and sometimes even in the presence of her family. Matters eventually came to a head three months into the relationship. Nick and Mandy had arranged a family dinner which Hollie and Maslin, Chloe and her boyfriend, were also to attend. But Maslin arrived at the restaurant an hour late and heavily intoxicated. He then proceeded to hurl abuse at everyone present, including Hollie's parents, restaurant staff, and other diners.

A short while after that incident, Hollie received an offer of working as a hairdresser aboard a cruise ship. The offer was contingent on her training for three months in Watford, north of London. That would mean moving away from her family, but her parents were thrilled by the idea. At least it meant that she would be away from Maslin and his malignant influence.

Unfortunately, Maslin was not about to give up his hold on Hollie that easily. Just days after she departed for Watford, he followed. He then began stalking her, keeping up his campaign of calls and texts and showing up at any bar or club that she went to with friends. Eventually, he simply wore her down and Hollie agreed to give their relationship another shot. She was just three weeks into her first stint aboard a cruise liner when he persuaded her to quit her dream job. He also pressured her to remain with him in London, rather than to return to Gloucester, where her family could dilute his influence over her.

Just weeks later, in August 2013, there was another troubling incident. Hollie and Maslin had been attending the Notting Hill Carnival when they became separated among the heaving crowds. For the next twenty minutes, Hollie tried desperately to find him, ignoring the constant beeping of her phone as he peppered her with texts. She was relieved when she finally spotted him among the crowd and made her way towards him. That relief, however, soon turned to fear and embarrassment. Maslin was furious that Hollie had not responded to his texts. In front of hundreds of horrified onlookers, he lashed out at her, beating her to the ground.

For Hollie, this beating, this public humiliation, was the last straw. The very next day, she quit her job and returned to the arms of her family in Gloucester. They, of course, were delighted to have her back home, and thrilled when she told them that she was done with Maslin.

If only it were that easy. By the following day, Maslin was back in Gloucester and back to employing his usual repertoire of intimidation tactics. There were the phone calls, the texts, the unexpected arrivals, the apparently heartfelt pleadings and the entirely genuine threats. He had also developed a new ploy. He informed Hollie that he would kill himself if she did not come back to him. His blood would then be on her hands.

Eventually, Hollie caved in and gave him yet another chance to prove his love for her. It was a mistake. Maslin soon reverted to old ways, and Hollie realized that he would never change, that he was probably incapable of changing. In January 2014, having endured 12 months of physical and emotional abuse, she told him that it was over and that there was no way back this time.

Maslin's response was to once again trot out his familiar playbook – texts, phone calls, threats against Hollie and her family, threats of suicide. Things eventually escalated to such a point that when Maslin asked her to meet with him on Valentine's Day 2014, Hollie agreed, hoping that she could appeal to him in person to move on with his life. He started the evening polite and attentive but soon became abusive when Hollie refused to "try again." Later that evening, when she was driving him home, he asked to use her cellphone. When Hollie said yes, he rifled through her handbag to retrieve the phone. The following day, she discovered that he'd taken her bank card while doing so and that he had already withdrawn several hundred pounds.

It was then that Hollie decided to go to the police, not just to report the theft but also the constant abuse, threats and intimidation. Her story was easy to verify. While she was talking to the officers, her phone barely stopped beeping, each message delivering a fresh threat, to kill her, to kill her family, to burn down their house.

Hollie stopped short of obtaining a restraining order against her former boyfriend. Had she done so, it would scarcely have made a difference. Maslin had already shown a total disregard for law and order, for common decency, for the needs of anyone bar himself. When he heard that Hollie had spoken to the police, he was furious. No one, however, could have anticipated what he did next.

On February 18, 2014, four days after her Valentine's Day meeting with Maslin, Hollie Gazzard was due to work an afternoon shift at a hairdressing salon in the Gloucester city center. That morning, she had a manicure and then had lunch before arriving at the salon in time for her first appointment. Colleagues said that she appeared her usual bubbly self.

Unbeknownst to Hollie, Maslin was also in town that afternoon, carrying a DVD player to a local pawn shop where he obtained £5 for it. His next stop was at a supermarket where he went straight to the kitchenware section and selected a large knife. At 5:47pm, he entered the salon where Hollie was working and walked directly towards her. Without saying a word, he punched her in the face then drew his knife and launched a frenzied attack, stabbing her 14 times in the space of under a minute. Then, as horrified customers cowered behind chairs and tables, he walked calmly from the salon, still holding the bloody murder weapon. Emergency services, summoned by a frantic call, were on the scene in minutes. They arrived too late to save Hollie who died two hours later from massive blood loss.

The race was now on to find Asher Maslin, who was considered a danger to the public and particularly to Hollie's family, who he had so often threatened. As they were being moved to secure locations, police began viewing CCTV footage and found that they could track Maslin's movements from the time he arrived on the Gloucester high street carrying his DVD player. He was seen entering the pawn shop, buying the knife, walking towards the salon, exiting and casually strolling away with the blood-stained knife still in his hand. He was also seen after the murder, leaving his house in fresh clothes and getting into a taxi. That allowed the police to track him to a friend's house where he was arrested eight hours later.

With such extensive evidence against him, much of it captured on CCTV or committed in the presence of eyewitnesses, Asher Maslin was left with little alternative but to plead guilty to murder at his trial. He showed no remorse during the proceedings and little emotion as he was sentenced to life in prison. The minimum tariff was set at 24 years. That means, of course, that he may one day be free, possibly as early as his mid-forties. Hollie's family, meanwhile, are condemned to a life without the daughter and sister they so loved.

Nightmare in Napa County

Back in the early '60s, Napa County, California, was a great place to raise a family. Long before the region achieved worldwide acclaim for its wine production, it was predominantly working class with a population of just 22,000. Crime was low and violent crime almost unheard of. Indeed, parents were quite happy to let their children walk to school and to play outside unattended. In March of 1963, all of that changed.

The Heskett family, Marvin, his wife Dorothy, and their nine children lived in a modest home at 2309 Main Street. Marvin was a salesman by trade and Dorothy a stay-at-home mom who had her hands full attending to her large brood, ranging in age from 17 years to five months. In early 1963, she had an additional burden to bear. Marvin had recently suffered a heart attack, his second in as many years, and was at home convalescing. He'd only recently been able to get up from his sickbed and walk around. Dorothy was genuinely concerned for his wellbeing.

And then, on Monday, March 25, all of those concerns were supplanted by a far greater crisis. That was the day that 5-year-old Doreen Heskett vanished.

Doreen had followed her normal routine that Monday, walking with her siblings to Lincoln Elementary School where she attended morning kindergarten classes. When class recessed at 11:30 a.m., the little girl walked home alone to eat lunch with her mother and younger siblings. At around 2 p.m., her friend Linda Ford arrived at the Heskett residence to play. Two hours later, Doreen asked her mother if she could go with Linda to her house to continue their play date. Dorothy, who was rushing to the grocery store at the time, said yes but told her to be home in time for dinner. She then watched as the girls set off together, Linda riding her bike and Doreen sitting on the carrier behind her.

What Dorothy didn't know was that the Ford family had recently moved. Once they'd been near neighbors of the Hesketts; now they lived a mile away on Sherman Avenue. It would have taken the girls around 15 minutes to get there, and they played for a mere 25 minutes before Mrs. Ford told Linda that it was time to take Doreen home. The girls left the Ford residence at around 4:40 p.m.

But Linda did not follow her mother's instructions. Rather than riding Doreen all the way back to Main Street, she let her off at the junction of Jefferson and Pueblo. Jefferson Street was, at that time, a major thoroughfare in Napa, a two-way stretch of blacktop that ran for five miles in either direction from the spot where Doreen now stood. In order to make her way home, the 5-year-old would have to walk east on Pueblo to where it intersected with Main. Instead, she started south on Jefferson. When Linda shouted out to her that she was going the wrong way, Doreen shouted back that she wanted to go past the school. Linda then mounted her bike and started pedaling for home.

As dinnertime approached, with no sign of Doreen, Dorothy Heskett decided to walk to the Ford residence to fetch her. It was only then that she discovered that the Fords had moved. She also realized that she did

not have their new phone number. Concerned now, she began walking
the neighborhood, hoping to encounter Doreen on her way home. Two
hours later, the frantic mother went to the police. They, in turn, phoned
the Ford residence and learned that Doreen had left hours earlier. A
search was then launched, with officers going door to door along the
route Doreen would have taken. They found nothing. The blonde-
haired, blue-eyed little girl had simply vanished.

Bloodhounds are an invaluable tool in police searches, and
neighboring Marin County, at that time, had one of the finest teams in
the state. Deputy Michael McLean and his hounds had received much
media attention for their success in locating murdered and missing
persons in the North Bay area. Napa Chief of Police Sherwood Munk
therefore put in a call and, within two hours, McLean and his
bloodhound Brandy were in Napa. The dog quickly picked up
Doreen's scent outside the Ford residence and followed it south down
to Jefferson Avenue and from there to the crossing signal in front of
Napa Union High School. There the trail came to an abrupt end.
Doreen had walked that far and no further, which meant that she had
probably gotten into a car at that spot.

Chief Munk's next move was to put out a statewide bulletin, asking
officers to be on the lookout for a little girl matching Doreen's
description. Over the days that followed, police departments in
California and neighboring states received a picture and description of
the missing girl. Munk also roped in the media, with Doreen's picture
appearing in newspapers and on television while local radio stations
issued appeals and regular bulletins.

In the meantime, ground searches were continuing in Napa and its surrounds. Seldom had the town seen such a community effort with thousands of volunteers mobilizing to help the police, service stations donating gasoline, and local housewives providing hot meals to the searchers and offering their help as babysitters. As the search spread to an area covering 100 square miles, personnel from Hamilton and Travis Air Force Bases got involved. A military helicopter was also seconded to the search, offering aerial surveillance.

And yet, this mammoth effort, involving over 3,000 individuals, came to nothing. After five days without success, Chief Munk was eventually forced to call an end to the search. The Chief was by now convinced that Doreen had been abducted by a sex offender and had sent his detectives out to question the nearly 100 individuals in the county who had a record for such crimes. Doreen's mother, meanwhile, clung to the desperate hope that her daughter had been taken by some childless woman who was desperate to have a child.

Over the days that followed, there were several reported sightings of Doreen, all of which turned out to be false. The Napa police had meanwhile concluded their survey of local deviants and had likewise failed to make a breakthrough. With all investigative avenues seemingly exhausted, Chief Munk decided in early April to call in the California Bureau of Criminal Identification and Investigation. Special Agent Sidney Jones was assigned and covered much the same ground as Napa PD, although he expanded the scope, running background checks on 290 registered sex offenders from Napa, Solano and Sonoma counties. The Napa cops also began working a new angle. They asked Dorothy and Marvin Heskett to take polygraphs which both parents did and passed.

There were more desperate measures, too. Chief Munk brought in a Los Angeles-based "psychic" to examine mugshots of convicted sex offenders. The woman detected no link between the men in the photographs and Doreen. Then the Heskett family issued a despairing, heart-felt appeal to the abductor via the Napa Register, begging him to return their daughter to them. It elicited no response. Doreen's fate remained a mystery, but it would not be so for very much longer.

On the morning of Thursday, November 21, 1963, a farmer named Earl Stewart was crossing a cow pasture on his property in South Napa when he stumbled upon the skeletal remains of a child. The remains were immediately assumed to be those of Doreen Heskett although the police were baffled by the location. The field had received particular attention during the search and had been covered on three separate occasions. It had also been surveyed by helicopter and had turned up nothing. Yet, here was the child's corpse and there was no doubt whatever that she had met with foul play.

The body lay face down, the right arm underneath it, the left arm outstretched with the fingers tightly clasped. A gaping hole in the skull pointed to blunt force trauma or perhaps a bullet wound. The condition of the clothes, with the child's panties around her knees, seemed to support the initial theory of a sexually motivated abduction.

But who had taken Doreen, raped her and killed her? Police attention went back to known sex offenders and to one man in particular. Claude Ray Jr. had a history of molesting young girls and had served time for sexual assault on a 7-year-old. At the time of Doreen's disappearance, he'd been working as a laborer on the Ghisletta Ranch, a property that adjoined Earl Stewart's farm, where the body had been found. And the Ray family lived within sight of the road crossing in front of Napa Union High School, where Doreen had disappeared. There was also a possibility that Doreen knew Claude Ray Jr., since his youngest daughter was in her kindergarten class.

Ray had already been questioned, of course, and had provided a seemingly unbreakable alibi. Now, with the discovery of Doreen's remains, he was hauled in again and repeated the story he'd told earlier. This time around, his delivery was not quite as convincing, but Ray was nonetheless sticking to it. He cockily challenged the detectives to charge him if they had any evidence. Since they did not, they were forced to let him go.

In late March of 1964, the remains found in Earl Stewart's field were formally identified as Doreen Heskett. Cause of death was more difficult to determine, though. The body had several fractures, but it was impossible to say whether these had been inflicted by the killer or if the corpse had been trampled by cattle while it lay in the field. What was certain, though, was that the body had not been in the field at the time of the initial police search. That meant that Doreen, whether dead or alive, was held at another location and only placed in the field after the search was called off. That, along with the indicators of sexual assault, marked this as a homicide, and it was now formally ruled as such.

But it was a homicide that, frustratingly, appeared to have little prospect of resolution. The police still regarded Claude Ray Jr. as their main suspect, but still they had no evidence against him. Then, on October 4, 1965, Ray provided them with a reminder of what he was capable of.

On that Monday morning, Claude Ray Jr. arranged with his estranged wife to drop his daughters, Jeanette, 9, and Renay, 7, at school. Later that day, the school phoned Mrs. Ray to ask why the girls had not showed up for classes. The concerned mother then phoned Ray and confronted him about the girls' whereabouts. When he insisted that he had dropped them off as agreed, Mrs. Ray called the police.

Responding to the call, Detective Sergeant Earl Randol immediately recognized Claude Ray Jr. as the prime suspect in the Heskett murder. As he had in that case, Ray now stuck to his guns, insisting that he'd dropped his daughters at Westwood Elementary and then driven to Mendocino to look for a job. Asked to provide details of where he had asked about work, Ray changed his story, now saying that he hadn't looked for work but had instead driven along the coastal road, pondering the state of his marriage. He then made an audacious statement which served only to heighten police suspicions. He expressed his concern that his daughters might have been taken by the same sex fiend who had killed Doreen Heskett.

On October 10, six days after Jeanette and Renay went missing, a man was collecting seashells with his family at Schooner Gulch, Mendocino County, when he came upon the body of a little girl, floating in the water. It was Renay Ray, dressed in a pink sweater and gray wool jumper but with her lower garments missing. An autopsy would later reveal that she had been sexually assaulted and that she had been killed by manual strangulation. The absence of water in the lungs proved that she was already dead when she was thrown into the sea.

Had Claude Ray Jr. really raped and murdered his own daughters? The police certainly believed him capable of such an atrocity, and the evidence supported it. Ray was immediately arrested for the murder. Despite his protestations of innocence, he was subsequently convicted and sentenced to life in prison. Sixteen years later, on July 11, 1983, he was found hanging in his cell, the victim of an apparent suicide.

Jeanette Ray's body was never found and so Ray was never charged with her murder and continued to deny it. He also maintained his innocence in the murder of Doreen Heskett, and the police were never able to bring charges against him. More than 50 years on, the case remains officially unsolved. There are few in law enforcement who doubt that Claude Ray Jr. was the man responsible.

Road Rage

It was a tragic scene, a quite obviously distressed woman appearing in front of the television cameras to appeal for help in catching her boyfriend's killer. The tale that 26-year-old Tracie Andrews had to tell was a terrifying one. She and 24-year-old Lee Harvey had visited a pub in Alvechurch, Worcestershire on the night of December 1, 1996. After leaving the bar, they'd been driving along a quiet country lane when a Ford Sierra had appeared behind them, the driver flashing the vehicle's lights. They had thought that he was trying to pass them, but instead, he started tailgating, forcing Lee to drive faster. A high-speed chase then ensued through the darkened streets, ending eventually when their pursuer forced them from the road in an area called Coopers Hill.

The driver, who Tracie described as a large man with bulging eyes, got out of his car and aggressively approached their vehicle. As he reached them, Lee flipped his door open and got out, but that proved to be a fatal mistake. The man was carrying a knife, and he immediately launched a frenzied attack on the unarmed Lee. Realizing what was happening, Tracie got out of the car and rounded it towards the attacker. She tried to pull him off Lee, but the man called her a slut and punched her in the face, knocking her to the ground. Then he resumed the knife attack, only breaking off when his blood-spattered victim lay dead on the ground. At that point, he walked casually to his car, got in, and drove away. By then, Lee Harvey was already dead. An autopsy would later reveal that he had been stabbed 37 times in the head, face, neck and back. The murder weapon was believed to be a small knife, possibly a penknife.

Tracie Andrews still bore the evidence of her encounter with her boyfriend's killer. She had cuts and bruises and sported a black eye during her television appearance. The emotional scars were in evidence too. Tracie sobbed uncontrollably through some of her testimony, at one point reaching for the hand of Maureen Harvey, Lee's mother, who was sitting beside her. But not everyone was convinced by her performance. Indeed, a body language expert suggested to police that she was lying. One of the key indicators was how Andrews appeared to grow in confidence as the news conference progressed. It was almost as though her self-belief increased as she saw that her story was being accepted.

And the West Midlands Police were beginning to have doubts themselves. Questioning residents near the site of the murder, they heard the same story over and over again. Witnesses had heard a man and a woman engaged in a furious argument. No one could recall hearing a third voice, or a car racing off in the way that Tracie had described. It was time to question their chief witness again, but when detectives arrived to interrogate Andrews, they found that she was in the hospital, having swallowed a handful of pills in an apparent suicide attempt.

Was that out of stress related to the attack? Was it out of guilt, or was it another ruse designed to throw investigators off track? The answers to those questions would have to wait until Tracie Andrews was sufficiently recovered to talk to detectives. In the meantime, they got to work looking for the staple of any murder investigation – motive. It wasn't long before they found one. Tracie Andrews, it appeared, was an extremely volatile woman.

Lee Harvey had met single mom Tracie at a night club in 1994 and had been immediately attracted to her. Tracie was blonde and pretty, although her looks were spoilt somewhat by a protruding jaw. She ran a perfume stall at a local market and had ambitions of becoming a model. Lee, who was working as a bus driver at the time, had similar aspirations. He also had a young daughter from a previous relationship which gave him and Tracie a lot in common. It wasn't long before the two of them were in a steady relationship.

But perhaps "steady" is the wrong adjective. As Lee was soon to discover, life with Tracie was no walk in the park. She was a bitter woman who harbored grudges against her family and acquaintances and often spouted bile about them, something the easygoing Lee found difficult to understand. That, however, was the least of his problems. He quickly learned that Tracie was jealous and possessive, that she expected to be the center of his world at all times, and that she was prone to fly off the handle if she felt that he wasn't paying her enough attention.

Those rages were not always confined to verbal rants. On more than one occasion, Lee was physically attacked, sometimes in public. And it didn't take much to set Tracie off. Once, she bit him in the neck for exchanging a few words with a barmaid. Another time, she hit him over the head with a bottle and punched him in the face for visiting "her" local nightclub during one of their many break-ups. Often, she threw him out of their shared apartment, tossing his clothes onto the lawn from an upstairs window. This treatment, apparently, was not isolated to Lee. According to neighbors, Tracie had ejected a succession of former boyfriends in similar fashion. Unlike them, however, Lee always came back, usually after staying at his parents' home for a few days. When his mother asked why he kept going back to Tracie, all Lee would say was that he loved her. That love, it appeared, had cost him his life.

Within days of the murder, the police had forensic evidence to back up their suspicions. Clumps of hair had been found in Lee Harvey's hands at the crime scene, and that hair had now been matched to Tracie Andrews. How could it have gotten there, other than during a vicious fight, a fight to the death, between the two of them? On December 7, detectives visited Tracie in her hospital bed and formally charged her with the murder of Lee Harvey. The assertion was that Lee and Tracie had argued in their car on the night of December 1 and that the argument had become so vicious that Lee had pulled over to the side of the road in order to prevent a crash. That was when Tracie drew a weapon (believed to be a Swiss Army-type utility knife) and attacked him, stabbing and slashing in a frenzy. When Lee finally collapsed from the cumulative effect of 37 stab wounds, she slit his throat and let him bleed to death at the roadside. She then invented the story about the irate driver to cover her tracks.

Tracie was incensed at the murder allegation and was still clinging to her road rage defense when the matter came to trial in July 1997 at the Birmingham Crown Court. Unfortunately for her, the jury gave her story about as much credence as the police had. Found guilty of murder, she was sentenced to life in prison with a minimum term of 14 years to be served before she became eligible for parole. She was sent to Foston Hall Prison in Derbyshire, still loudly protesting her innocence and declaring a miscarriage of justice.

But by April 1999, Andrews appeared to have had a change of heart. In a letter to her attorney, she finally admitted that it was she who had killed Lee Harvey. She insisted, however, that she had acted in self-defense after he had attacked her. She would later repeat her admission of guilt during one-on-one counseling with a prison psychologist. Cynics suggested at the time that she was only confessing to ensure that she would be eligible for parole at the earliest opportunity.

While serving her sentence, Tracie Andrews continued to court controversy. She befriended notorious fellow inmates like Jane Andrews (the former personal dresser of Lady Sarah Ferguson, who was convicted of bludgeoning and stabbing her lover to death) and Maxine Carr (who helped her lover, Ian Huntley, cover up the Soham murders). Andrews also sparked outrage when she received cosmetic surgery (paid for by the State) to correct her jutting jawline. She was in the news again in 2011, when she was photographed shopping for perfume and beauty products in York while out on day release.

And that was just the prelude to what Lee's parents had been fearing since the trial. In January 2012, 42-year-old Tracie Andrews (now calling herself Tia Carter) walked free from prison. She had served just 14 years for the brutal slaying of Lee Harvey.

Murder and Miranda

On a chilly November morning in 2013, a resident of Sunbury, Pennsylvania, looked out of her kitchen window and was shocked to see a man lying on the hard concrete of the alley that bounded her property. She went out to see if she could offer assistance, but just one look and she decided that this was a matter for the authorities. The man did not appear to be breathing and there was blood on the ground and on his clothing. The woman punched 911 into her phone and called it in.

To the officers who responded to the call, it was immediately clear that the man had met with foul play. Not only had he suffered multiple stab wounds, but there were marks on his throat, indicating that he had also been strangled. The ligature that had caused those marks was found when the officers rolled the man over. It was a length of electrical cable. And there was an even more valuable clue, lying just a short distance from the body – a cellphone. Officers bagged the phone. Since the dead man was carrying no identification, he was checked into the morgue as a John Doe.

But that anonymity would not last long. Back at the station, detectives were trying to get past the cellphone's pass code when they received an incoming call. It was from a woman who identified herself as Coleen LaFerrara and said she was trying to find her husband, 42-year-old Troy LaFerrara. According to Coleen, Troy had gone to dinner at his parents' home the previous evening and hadn't been seen since. Detectives then asked for her address and visited her at home in the neighboring town of Selinsgrove. There, they delivered the devastating news. Troy had been found. Murdered.

Tracking the dead man's last movements, detectives next called at his parents' home where they learned that Troy had eaten dinner, then worked on the computer for a while before leaving just after eight. One of the officers then checked the computer's browser history and learned something about Troy LaFerrara that neither his wife nor his parents knew. He was living a double life, trawling Craigslist under various aliases, looking for sex partners.

Might one of those partners have killed him? The detectives had by now handed LaFerrara's cellphone over to tech experts who had been able to bypass the security code. Scrolling through the latest activity, officers immediately picked up a number that LaFerrara had called several times on the night he died. That number belonged to a young woman named Miranda Barbour.

On November 13, 2013, investigators called at the Selinsgrove address shared by 19-year-old Miranda Barbour, her 22-year-old husband Elyette, and Miranda's two-year-old daughter. Miranda went willingly to Sunbury police headquarters where she provided an alibi for the night of the murder. According to her, she'd been out with her husband, celebrating his birthday. After a babysitter verified the alibi, Miranda was allowed to leave.

Later that day, the police had a break in the case when they found Troy LaFerrara's pickup at the Susquehanna Valley Mall in Hummels Wharf, Pennsylvania. The vehicle itself yielded little in the way of forensic evidence. The mall's surveillance footage, however, was a different story. It showed LaFerrara pulling up beside a dark-colored SUV then getting out of his truck and into the passenger seat of the other vehicle. Then the SUV reversed and pulled away.

Unfortunately, the quality of the picture wasn't clear enough for detectives to make out the driver or the license plate. Footage obtained from the mall's Wal-Mart store produced better results. In it, a man could be seen in the backseat of the SUV, a man who looked suspiciously like Elyette Barbour. Elyette was also picked up on the department store's internal surveillance cameras. He is seen walking up and down the aisles picking items from the shelves, items that included scrubbing brushes, bleach and other cleaning materials.

On December 2, 2013, Miranda Barbour was asked to come down to the station for a second interview. Asked whether she knew a man named Troy LaFerrara, she barely missed a beat in saying that she did not. The officers then revealed that they had found messages to and from her number on LaFerrara's phone at which point Miranda suddenly recalled that she had exchanged texts with him. She maintained, however, that she had never met him in person. She explained that she offered a service via Craigslist where she connected with lonely men who needed someone to talk to. She insisted that she only offered companionship and a sympathetic ear and did not sleep with any of the men. Her price for this service? Between $100 and $850.

The detectives found it difficult to believe that anyone would pay $850 just to talk, but they nonetheless allowed Miranda to continue with her story. She admitted that she had agreed to meet LaFerrara at the Susquehanna Valley Mall on the night of November 11 but said that she had become nervous about the meeting and had decided not to go. Instead, she and her husband had driven to a strip club in Harrisburg where they'd spent the evening celebrating his birthday.

The problem with that story was that the police had surveillance footage of Troy LaFerrara getting into Miranda's SUV. Still, they did not share that information with their suspect at this stage. Instead, they got a search warrant for her vehicle. Despite the obvious effort that had been made to clean it, the search turned up a large patch of blood under the passenger seat. That blood would ultimately be matched to the murder victim. Before those results were received, however, Miranda Barbour showed up at a Selinsgrove police station with yet another revision to her story.

This time, Miranda cut straight to the chase. She admitted that she'd killed Troy LaFerrara but denied that she'd murdered him. She'd acted in self-defense, she insisted, after LaFerrara had attacked her. In this version of events, she'd met LaFerrara at the mall and gone for a drive with him. Along the route, he had asked her to pull over on a dark street. Then he'd placed his hand between her thighs and had started fondling her. Miranda was afraid that she was about to be raped. She kept a knife for protection in the storage pocket of the door and now she reached for it. Then, according to her, she blacked out. When she came to, she was plunging the knife repeatedly into LaFerrara's chest. LaFerrara, by then, was already dead.

Miranda had panicked. Afraid of what would happen if she reported the killing to the police, she'd driven her vehicle into an alley and dragged LaFerrara from the passenger seat. Then she'd driven home and told Elyette what had happened, and together they had cleaned up the car. Having done that, they'd driven to the strip club in Harrisburg in order to establish an alibi.

Miranda had delivered her self-defense story in convincing fashion. She might well have been believed but for two things. Firstly, the police knew from surveillance footage that Elyette had been in the car with her. Secondly, LaFerrara had not only been stabbed, he'd also been strangled. Miranda had made no mention of that. Quite obviously, she was trying to shield Elyette.

Her efforts, though, would be in vain. On December 6, three days after Miranda was taken into custody, Elyette surrendered himself to the Pennsylvania State Police and admitted his involvement in the murder. His telling of events probably comes closest to the truth.

According to Elyette, LaFerrara had been lured via Craigslist with the express intention of killing him. The motive? Miranda had often spoken to her husband about the people she had killed and how murder filled her with an immense feeling of power. Elyette had wanted to experience that for himself. On the night that Miranda picked up LaFerrara, Elyette had been hiding in the back seat. The idea was that

Miranda would drive to a secluded spot and then speak a pre-arranged phrase ("Have you seen the stars tonight?"). That would be the signal to launch the attack. However, Elyette had frozen when his wife had spoken the words. It was only after Miranda started stabbing LaFerrara that he had joined in, looped the cord around his victim's neck and started strangling him.

Elyette and Miranda Barbour would ultimately plead guilty to murder in order to avoid the death penalty. Each would be sentenced to life in prison without parole. But something in Elyette's confession still intrigued investigators. He had said that his wife had often spoken to him about the people she'd killed and how murder gave her a feeling of power. Did that mean that there were other victims? Was it possible that 19-year-old Miranda Barbour was a serial killer?

Miranda was certainly doing nothing to dispel that notion. From behind bars, she had already given an interview to a journalist in which she'd claimed to have committed between 22 and 100 murders over six years, the first when she was just 13 years old and a member of a satanic cult.

Looking into Miranda's background, the police learned that she had been born in Alaska and had suffered sexual abuse as a child at the hands of her uncle. He had subsequently been convicted and sentenced to 19 years in jail, but by then the damage was already done. Deeply affected by her ordeal, Miranda had begun drinking and doing drugs before she was even into her teens. By thirteen, she'd fallen in with a group of teenaged Satanists. As the only girl in the group, she had been treated as a sexual toy, passed from one boy to the next. At 16, she fell pregnant and that, at least, had a positive effect. She decided to get her life together, moved from Alaska to North Carolina and got a job as a cashier in a supermarket. It was in North Carolina that she met Elyette Barbour. Shortly after that meeting, Elyette abandoned his girlfriend and baby and moved with Miranda to Pennsylvania. They married there in October 2013. Just three weeks after the wedding, the couple would set up their deadly rendezvous with Troy LaFerrara.

So what are we to make of Miranda Barbour's serial killer claims? Despite an intensive investigation, the police found nothing to back them up. What is more likely is that Miranda harbored a deep-seated desire to strike back at society for the wrong she had suffered as a child. This was perhaps why she'd told Elyette that she only killed "bad people." Had she somehow managed to avoid detection for the LaFerrera murder, there is a very good chance that she would have killed again. Thankfully, she will never get the opportunity.

Death of a Cheater

Yves Bourgade was a womanizer. Everyone knew that, not least because Yves boasted openly about his many conquests. He even discussed the details of his sexual exploits at dinner parties with his wife Florence sitting across the table from him. And while his X-rated stories embarrassed some of the dinner guests, Florence sat quietly and made no comment. In France, affairs are usually accepted as part of the marital landscape.

Yves and Florence had met in the mid-nineties and had tied the knot in 1997. The 14 years they had spent together had been good ones, producing three children, two boys and a girl. For all his dalliances, Yves was fun to be around, the life of any party, always ready to have a good time. Florence loved that about him. He was also a good provider who ran a small but profitable business as a building contractor.

Lately, however, friends and family had noticed some strain on the relationship. Yves had always been a heavy drinker, but now he was out most nights, usually returning in an inebriated state in the early morning hours. His business had suffered as a result and, with it, the couple's finances. In the last year, they'd had to sell the large villa they had owned in Moigny-sur-École, 36 miles south of Paris, and move into rented accommodation. There, neighbors often noticed raised and angry voices coming from the house at all hours of the night. And it was easy to decipher what the arguments were about – money, or rather the lack of it. Yves's lifestyle had put the family heavily into debt.

The arguments were not the only outward indicator of trouble at home. Florence had always been a vivacious, fun-loving woman, but lately she seemed morose, depressed. Whereas she had normally been outgoing and chatty, she now spent social events ensconced in some dark corner with barely a word to say to anyone. Dark rings under her eyes were the mark of someone who was having trouble sleeping at night, and indeed Florence had recently visited her family physician and obtained a prescription for the powerful sedative, Zopiclone. That was on Tuesday, February 25, 2004.

The following morning at around 7 a.m., Florence's sister Pauline, who lived in the neighboring town of Barbizon, some ten miles away, received a phone call. Florence was on the line, sounding somewhat stressed and asking for a favor. She said that Yves had arrived home drunk as usual and that the two of them had gotten into an argument. Yves was being verbally abusive, and she did not want their children to witness his behavior. Could she therefore send the children over for a couple of days? Pauline, of course, said yes. Florence then thanked her and said that her next-door neighbor would drop the kids off on her way to work.

Florence made at least one more call that morning. It was to her husband's only employee to inform him that he should not come in to work that day. "Yves has blown a fuse" was the only explanation she provided before hanging up.

Later that day, towards evening, Florence made another call to her sister, giving Pauline an update on her ongoing battle with Yves. "He's gone," she said with barely a shred of emotion in her voice. She then went on to explain that Yves had abandoned her and the children for his latest lover. According to her, a gray Renault Scenic had pulled up in front of the house at around four o'clock that afternoon. Yves had walked out to the vehicle, carrying his clothes in two black trash bags. He'd then gotten in and the car had driven away. Florence had seen a young, blonde woman at the wheel, but it wasn't anyone she recognized. "I don't care anyway," she said coldly. "Good riddance!"

The following day, Florence phoned Yves's sister and told her a similar story. Her sister-in-law urged her to find Yves and persuade him to return home. Florence refused to do so, but by the following day, Yves's family had urged her to report Yves missing.

The French police have a unique approach to such cases. Whereas reports of missing children are given immediate and coordinated attention, an adult must be missing for two months before an investigation is launched. This, of course, does not apply where there is evidence of foul play, but in the case of Yves Bourgade, there was none. It appeared that the serial philander had indeed abandoned his family, an offence which, under French law, rendered him liable for prosecution and a possible two-year jail term. The gendarmes, therefore, asked Florence to let them know if Yves return home. They took no further action.

On Friday, February 27, 48 hours since Yves had left home, a cyclist was wending his way through the Grands Avaux Forest, some six miles north of Moigny-sur-École. It was not the ideal weather for outdoor activities, 21 degrees and with a heavy fog hanging in the treetops, but this nature enthusiast loved the aromatic scent of damp vegetation, of chestnut, oak, and acacia. Except that now, his nostrils were being assailed by another smell, something distinctly unpleasant. Dismounting his bicycle, the man went to investigate and soon came upon the source of the stink – a canvas-covered bundle lying on the ground in a clearing. The cyclist decided on the spot that he did not want to know what lurked under the sheeting. Instead, he got back onto his bike and went for the police.

Soon a contingent of gendarmes had arrived on the scene, and it did not take them long to establish that the canvas concealed a corpse. The body was missing its head, hands and feet, and it had also been burned in an apparent effort to conceal the victim's identity. The area was immediately closed off and subjected to a grid search for evidence. The body, meanwhile, was photographed and then removed to the morgue for examination. As it was lifted, a detective noticed a cigarette butt that had been lying under it and bagged that as evidence. The corpse and the cigarette butt were later subjected to DNA analysis in an attempt to establish the victim's identity.

It would be three months before the results of those DNA tests were available. In the meantime, the police were still none the wiser as to the identity of the victim or to how he had died. The burning of the body made it impossible to determine the cause or date of death, although there were some clues as to how he'd met his end. Fractured vertebrae and a ruptured liver pointed to violent blows inflicted on the body; the presence of a non-benzodiazepine sleeping pill suggested that he might have been passed out when those blows were delivered. Breakfast cereal in the stomach hinted at the means by which the sedative might have been ingested.

While all of this was going on, Florence Bourgade was ignoring all calls by her husband's family to launch a private search for Yves. Florence, it appeared, had drawn a line under that chapter. She was moving on, obliterating all evidence of her husband's existence. First, she closed down Yves's business. Then she sold his cars and his clothes and canceled his cell phone subscription. She began making plans to move away from the area, sold off items of furniture from their house and embarked on a major spring clean of their rented property. This involved ripping up carpets in the bedroom and scrubbing down walls and floors. When Yves's family complained about her selling off his stuff, she said that she needed the money to feed her children and also to pay off the considerable debts that Yves had run up. As for the cleaning, she wanted to leave the house in a "fit state" before moving out.

In May 2004, after three months of waiting, the police finally had the DNA results. However, there was disappointment when they looked for a match on the national database – there was none. Neither was there a match to the DNA lifted from the cigarette butt, although they did glean one snippet of information – the genetic material was from a woman.

The lack of a DNA match was a setback to the investigation. With nothing else to go on, detectives reverted to good old legwork and decided to follow up recent missing person reports from the region. That, of course, brought them to Florence Bourgade's door, and the responses she gave to their questions must have aroused suspicion because the officers asked her to accompany them to the station. There, she was asked outright if she'd murdered her husband, and she emphatically denied it, saying that she had neither the "physical nor emotional strength" to commit murder. She then agreed to provide a sample for DNA analysis and was allowed to leave.

Swabs were later also obtained from Yves's family so that a comparison could be made with the headless, handless, footless corpse that had been found in the Grands Avaux forest. This time, the tests took only a few days. The body matched the DNA profiles of Yves's family. The DNA found on the cigarette was a match to Florence Bourgade. On June 1, Florence was arrested on suspicion of murdering her husband.

Florence, of course, denied any involvement in Yves's death. She continued to insist that he had run away with a lover. She also had answers to everything the police threw at her regarding her disposal of Yves's assets and her suspicious house-cleaning activities. When detectives asked if she had ever been prescribed sleeping pills, she admitted that she had, although she didn't remember the brand name (the police by now knew that it was Zopiclone, which has a similar chemical make-up to the drug found in Yves's body). When she was questioned about power tools that were missing from Yves's work premises, including an electric saw, she said that she had "probably sold them" but couldn't provide a bill of sale. Questioned about a discrepancy in her early evidence regarding the time Yves had left the house, she said that she had been in shock. "He'd just told me that he was leaving me for a 25-year-old woman," she said.

The police did not believe a word of it. They had now built up a likely timeline for the crime, one that fit the evidence far better than Florence's version of events. They believed Florence had drugged Yves by putting Zopiclone into a bowl of cereal she gave him to eat. After he passed out, she bludgeoned him to death and then cut off his head, hands and feet with his own electric chain saw. She'd then driven the body to the forest and burned it to further hamper identification. While doing so, she had accidentally dropped the cigarette butt which the police had later found. She'd then returned home and, after sending the children to her sister, she had gone to work cleaning up the crime scene. She had ripped up carpet, disposed of a bloodstained mattress, and scrubbed down walls and floors.

It was a thorough effort, and despite many hours spent sifting through the local municipal dump, the police would never find the missing carpet and mattress (or, for that matter, Yves's head, hands and feet). But regardless of how thoroughly Florence had scrubbed down the house, she could not hide the presence of blood from a formidable tool in the investigative arsenal – Luminol. This compound of hydragine and hydrogen peroxide emits a blue-green glow when it is exposed to the hemoglobin in blood under a fluorescent light. When it was applied to a wall in Yves and Florence's bedroom, the surface lit up like a Christmas tree. Positive results were also obtained from the bathtub, bathroom wall, and a fire extinguisher found in the entrance hall of the house. Based on these results, Florence was formally charged with murder.

Florence Bourgade would spend 31 months incarcerated at Fleury-Merogis jail before her trial eventually rolled around at the Court of Justice in Évry on Monday, January 15, 2007. She entered a plea of not guilty and had a rebuttal for every allegation made by the prosecution. Regarding the blood found in her home, she insisted that Yves often came home bloodied and battered after getting involved in drunken brawls; as for the cigarette found at the crime scene, she said that the police had planted it there. Yet when she was called to the stand herself, she refused to answer any questions, responding to each with a terse: "I have no answer to give."

That strategy did her no good in the end. After retiring for just two hours, the jury returned with a verdict of guilty of assassination (the French judicial term for first-degree murder). She was sentenced to 20 years in prison – four years more than the prosecutor had asked for. That sentence was later reduced to 15 years on appeal, but it still meant a decade and a half behind bars for Florence Bourgade.

Paper Roses

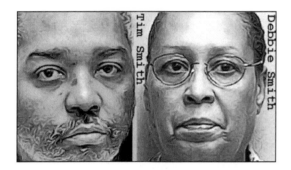

Councilor Gail Smith was an active and well-liked woman in Berryville, Virginia. So when the councilwoman wasn't seen around town over a period of four days in July 2009, a police cruiser was dispatched to her residence to check on her. Patrolman Greg Frenzel, one of only nine officers on the Berryville force, responded to the call. Getting no reply when he rang the doorbell, he peered through a window and spotted the councilwoman lying on the floor. Frenzel then entered the residence and immediately picked up the putrid stench of decomposition. Gail Smith was dead, her corpse already bloated in the summer heat. Frenzel immediately called it in.

It wasn't long before crime scene tape had been strung out, securing the scene. Then investigators from the Berryvale police and Clarke County Sheriff's Department got to work, trying to determine the facts of the 60-year-old councilwoman's death. Although there was a small amount of dried blood on the floor, investigators assumed that this was from striking her head when she'd fallen. And since there was no sign of a break-in or struggle, the initial impression was that Smith had died of a heart attack.

One thing puzzled the detectives, though. Scattered around the body were the remnants of a bouquet of paper flowers. Those who knew Gail Smith knew that she was a keen gardener with a love of living, growing things. The fake flowers didn't make sense. Why were they there? Had someone other than Gail brought them into the house? Questions such as those would have to wait until a definite cause of death was determined.

The body was removed to the morgue where the autopsy produced a result that the police were not expecting. Gail Smith had not died of natural causes. She'd been shot in the head with a .22 handgun, the weapon held so close that it had left powder burns on her scalp. The bullet was still lodged in the skull, but unfortunately it was badly damaged, making ballistic testing impossible. Based on the state of the corpse, the coroner estimated that Smith had been shot on July 26, four days before her body was found. The question was: Who would have wanted to kill the much-loved town councilor?

As police began looking into possible motives, they focused first on Smith's political life. Had the outspoken councilwoman ruffled someone's feathers? Enough for them to want her dead? Apparently not. While some of Smith's fellow councilors admitted that they didn't agree with her on every issue, they insisted that she was a respected and well-liked colleague whose sense of civic duty was very much admired.

Next, suspicion fell on the driver of a white pickup who had been going door to door in the neighborhood offering his power-washing services. Several neighbors had been approached by the man, and they also remembered that his truck had been parked in Gail Smith's driveway on the day of her death. The man had told prospective clients that he worked for a local contractor, and so detectives headed to a nearby construction site. There they learned that the man they were looking for was a local hustler named Randall Franklin. They learned something else, too. Franklin had not been back to work since the day of Gail Smith's murder.

This looked like a promising lead. Franklin was quickly tracked to a bar in nearby Charlestown. He was far from co-operative, although he did admit that he'd been at Smith's house on July 26. He'd offered to power wash her house, he said, she'd declined and so he'd left. With no way of proving otherwise, the police were forced to let it drop.

With leads rapidly running out on them, the police began looking into Gail Smith's background. They learned that she had been born in Brooklyn, New York, and had moved to Berryville after retiring from her career as a flight attendant in 1993. She had a brother and sister living in Farmville, some three hours away, and a father who was in a nursing home in nearby Harrisonburg. In fact, Gail had originally moved to Virginia so that she could be near to her father. According to her brother Tim, they were a close-knit family. He and Gail's sister Debbie were devastated by her passing.

The day after that interview with Tim Smith, detectives got a call from Gail's lawyer which seemed to cast doubt on some of the things Tim had told them. It appeared that the Smith siblings were not quite as close as he'd claimed. In fact, they had been involved in a bitter legal dispute. Gail had lodged a petition to be named as her father's legal guardian, a move that would have given her control over his reported three-quarter-million-dollar estate. Tim and Debbie were opposing her through the courts. Might this dispute have been a motive for murder?

To find out, investigators began delving into the pasts of Tim and Debbie Smith. Debbie came up clean, but in Tim's case, there was an extensive rap sheet involving arrests and jail time for fraud, theft, and other property crimes. Still, there was nothing to indicate a history of violence, and Tim was in his sixties and in poor health, requiring a cane or a wheelchair to move around. He could not have shot his sister. It looked like another dead end.

Four months passed. Then, out of the blue, the police got a break in the case. In November 2009, an inmate at the Farmville Detention Center contacted investigators and said that he had information on the Gail Smith murder. According to the man, Tim Smith had approached him a year earlier and asked him to murder his sister. Smith had offered $2,000 for the job and had said that he wanted it done with rattlesnake venom, the effects of which would simulate a heart attack. The man had declined the offer.

Tim Smith was adamant that the inmate's story was a fabrication. Nonetheless, he was taken into custody and charged with conspiracy to commit murder and solicitation to murder. He swore that he would fight to prove his innocence. By the time the matter came to court, however, Smith appeared to have had a change of heart. He approached the prosecutor for a deal and offered a plea of 'no contest' in exchange for a two-year jail term.

Perhaps Smith thought that this would appease the Berryville police and cause them to back off from the murder inquiry. If anything, it had the opposite effect. Investigators were now more convinced than ever that Smith was involved. Except that he couldn't have been the shooter himself due to his physical condition. He must have had an accomplice.

Tracking down that accomplice now became the primary focus of the investigation. Detectives began looking at Smith's cellphone records and soon picked up an anomaly. Several calls had been made to Tim from a specific phone on the weekend that Gail was killed. Then, after the murder, the calls from that number abruptly stopped. Tracking the phone itself, investigators found that it was a pre-paid unit, a "burner" in street talk. They found also that the phone's user had traveled from Farmville to Berryville on the day before Gail was shot. All of the calls made from the phone were to Tim Smith. All except one. The last call was to a pizza parlor in Farmville.

Calling on the pizzeria, detectives were able to confirm that a pizza had indeed been ordered from that phone number. They were also given the address that the delivery had gone to. That turned out to be a neat bungalow in a respectable neighborhood. The homeowner, Gladys Jackson, appeared genuinely perplexed by the officers' questions, insisting that she never ordered in. Then, as an afterthought, she said that her granddaughter had been living with her until recently and might have made the call. That snippet of information sent the officers to an apartment on the other side of town, where Ashley Jackson lived with her boyfriend Tony Sharpe.

Tony and Ashley were questioned separately by police. Neither was very helpful, although both admitted that they knew Tim Smith. Tony claimed that he was a former neighbor but denied that Tim had ever given him a pre-paid cellphone. Ashley said that Tony sometimes did odd jobs for Tim. According to Tony, he knew about Gail Smith's murder only because she was Tim's sister. He denied having anything to do with it. Nothing that the officers said could get him to deviate from his story.

The case had reached another impasse. Investigators were certain that Tim Smith was involved, and they strongly suspected that Tony Sharpe had been the shooter. The problem was that they lacked the evidence to prove it. In August 2012, Tim Smith walked out of Chesterfield Correctional Facility having completed his conspiracy sentence. At this stage, it seemed likely that he would remain a free man.

And that might well have been the case had Smith been able to keep his mouth shut. But he just had to boast about how clever he was in getting away with murder. In January 2013, a man named Darryl Young contacted the Berryville police. According to Young, Smith had admitted the murder to him, saying that he'd paid a man named Tony Sharpe $1,900 to carry out the hit. But Tim wasn't the only member of the Smith family who was involved in the conspiracy. Debbie had been in on it from the start. It was she who had come up with the idea of the bogus flower delivery. In fact, she'd given Tony Sharpe the money to buy the flowers.

Now the fake flowers found at the scene made sense to investigators. It also proved to them that Darryl Young was telling the truth, since that particular detail had never been made public.

In March 2013, detectives brought in Ashley Young, the now ex-girlfriend of suspected shooter Tony Sharpe. Previously, Ashley had been reluctant to talk. But with a possible conspiracy charge hanging over her head, she broke down and admitted that Tony had mysteriously come into a large sum of money in the days after Gail's death. He'd told her that Tim had given it to him but had initially refused to divulge what he'd done to earn it. Pressed on the issue, he had eventually admitted that he had killed Tim's sister.

Tim Smith and Tony Sharpe were taken into custody that same day. Under interrogation, the younger man quickly cracked and admitted that he was the shooter. He said that he'd gained access to Gail's house by posing as a flower deliveryman. Once inside, he'd pushed her to the floor and placed the gun against her temple. He'd shot her as she begged for her life. Tim had paid him $1,900 for the hit, he said. He also testified that Debbie had been an active participant in the conspiracy.

Debbie Smith would ultimately strike a deal with investigators, agreeing to testify against her brother in exchange for all charges, bar the relatively minor one of perjury, being dropped against her. She was sentenced to four to seven years. Tony Sharpe also agreed to testify against Tim, accepting a term of 25 years as part of the plea bargain. As for Tim, he initially refused to speak to prosecutors but wilted when he learned that his co-conspirators had turned on him. His guilty plea earned him a 23-year prison term. Given his age and poor state of health, he will likely die behind bars.

A Monster in Our Midst

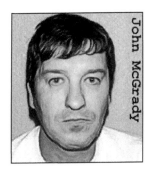

John McGrady

During the early 2000s, police officers in the south London suburb of Catford dreaded getting calls from the Milford Towers housing estate. The area was a hotbed of petty crime, with break-ins, assaults, drug dealing, and incidents of domestic violence reported on a regular basis. And officers were often met with abuse, sometimes even outright violence, when they responded to calls. Still, the hard-pressed officers of the local precinct had never seen anything like this. The initial report had been of a "seriously injured man" supposedly lying in a stairwell. That, however, would prove to be false. The truth was far, far worse.

Rochelle Holness was a 15-year-old schoolgirl who lived close to Milford Towers with her parents and brothers. Living in such close proximity to the notorious estate was far from ideal, but the Holness family was a tight-knit unit who looked out for each other, and Rochelle was a sensible young girl who knew how to avoid trouble. Her parents were, therefore, not at all worried when, on the evening of Sunday, September 25, 2005, she announced that she was going to a call box to phone her boyfriend. They were likewise unconcerned when she failed to return home. They assumed that she had met up with friends and decided to sleep over. She'd done so before and they trusted her.

But Monday morning brought good reason for alarm. Rochelle's boyfriend called and said that he had neither seen her nor heard from her. That sent the family to all corners of the estate, knocking on doors and asking if anyone might have seen Rochelle. Nobody had, but still the family wavered in reporting her disappearance to the police. It was only on Tuesday that they filed a report. The police then took up the search but fared no better. The denizens of Milford Towers were naturally suspicious of law enforcement and reluctant to talk to them.

By Wednesday morning, September 28, Rochelle had been missing three days, and despite their efforts, neither the police nor the Holness family had any idea as to what had happened to her. Unbeknownst to them, the mystery was about to unravel itself... in tragic circumstances. That same morning, a 999 caller reported that there was an injured man lying in a stairwell at Milford Towers. An ambulance was dispatched but found no one at the scene. What they found instead was a shopping cart, heavily-laden with plastic garbage bags. What was inside those bags was truly horrific.

The only way to describe it was that Rochelle Holness had been butchered, her body cut into five pieces and then packed into bags and loaded into the shopping cart. The position of the cart, beside a garbage chute, suggested to police that the killer had been in the process of dumping the body parts and had probably been interrupted. The pathologist would later determine that a hacksaw had been used to dismember the corpse and that the killer had displayed some skill in doing so. Death, however, had been caused by asphyxiation, probably due to manual strangulation. Although there were no clear signs of sexual assault, this was deemed the most likely motive. Rochelle had been carrying nothing of value save for the change she needed for the telephone.

Right from the start, investigators believed that the person responsible for Rochelle's murder lived on the housing estate, more than likely in the very tower block where the body had been found. They reasoned that the killer had accosted Rochelle as she was trying to make her call and had forced her, probably at knifepoint, into his apartment. There he'd sexually assaulted her, or perhaps had been thwarted in his efforts to do so because Rochelle had put up a fight. Either way, he'd strangled her to death, then set about dismembering the corpse. Since the police had found nothing during their earlier searches of the area, they reasoned that the body parts had remained in the killer's apartment for three days before he tried to dispose of them. Having been disturbed while trying to do so, he'd left behind the evidence of his grisly workmanship and had fled.

It was a workable theory. And yet, despite Rochelle disappearing at 7 p.m. on a mild Sunday evening, no one appeared to have seen or heard anything. In any other case, the police might have thought that the residents of Milford Towers were holding out on them, but not in this one. The murder had traumatized the locals. A killer was living among them and they wanted him caught. If anyone had seen or heard anything, the police were confident that they would have come forward. They were certain of something else, too. The person who had committed this crime was not a first-timer. He would very likely have a criminal record, if not for murder, then at least for sexual assault.

Although they couldn't know it at the time, the police were right on just about every assumption they had made thus far. The man they sought was indeed living under their noses in Milford Towers, and he did indeed have a criminal record. His name was John McGrady, he was 47 years old and making his living as a handyman. He was also a heavy drinker and had committed most of the countless sexual assaults that peppered his rap sheet while under the influence.

McGrady's record of violent knifepoint rapes went back to his teens, when he broke into an apartment in Clapham, London and threatened the female occupant with a pair of scissors before raping her. McGrady had never been charged with that offence, but he was arrested three times for rape during the early eighties. Incredibly, he managed to convince all three juries that the sex was consensual, even though he was wearing a ski-mask and wielding a knife when he attacked his victims.

McGrady's luck was about to run out, though. In 1983, he was charged with false imprisonment after abducting a young woman at knifepoint as she stepped off a bus. That earned him five years behind bars but prison appears to have had little remedial effect on John McGrady. He had barely been released when he was in trouble again, this time for the knifepoint rapes of two 19-year-olds. At trial, McGrady again trotted out his "consensual sex" defense. This jury, however, was less gullible and sentenced him to ten years in prison.

John McGrady walked free from his latest period of incarceration in 1997, the same year that Britain introduced a sex offenders register. Since McGrady's offences pre-dated the introduction of the register, his name was not recorded, and that, perhaps, gave him the freedom to prey on other young women. If he did so (and the police are almost certain that he did), he was never caught. During that time, he lived an apparently quiet and near reclusive life, the latter part of it at Milton Towers, where he would commit his horrendous mutilation murder.

The murder of Rochelle Holness was by now big news in the British press, with the tabloids taking graphic reportage to a level that was disrespectful to the victim and deeply distressing to her family. In one particularly distasteful article, The Sun newspaper reported that Rochelle had been gagged, strapped to a kitchen table and dismembered while she was still alive. The Press Complaints Commission was quick to uphold a complaint by Rochelle's parents and the police equally swift to issue a statement debunking the story. Rochelle had been strangled, they said, and had likely died within an hour of her abduction.

But how close were investigators to catching her killer? The police were following two main avenues of inquiry. The first was classic legwork, with officers going door to door, interviewing residents. The second involved identifying convicted sex offenders living in the area. Either of those paths might eventually have led to John McGrady. But McGrady was about to do something to accelerate the process. On September 28, he decided to kill himself.

In truth, it was a feeble attempt. The man who so readily wielded a knife against defenseless women, who could butcher a corpse on his kitchen table, could not bring himself to cut very deeply into his own wrists. He had, however, left behind a note for his girlfriend, and in it he admitted to killing and dismembering Rochelle Holness. Horrified, the woman took the note directly to the police.

McGrady was arrested on September 29, 2005, four days after he killed Rochelle. After treatment for superficial cuts, he was charged with her murder. As police began looking into his background, they discovered some interesting facts about the Belfast-born killer. His brother, Kevin, had been an IRA assassin, and it had been while visiting him in London during the 1970s that McGrady had committed his first rape. They learned also that McGrady had trained as a butcher, which perhaps explained his expert dissection of his victim's corpse.

John McGrady was convicted of murder at London's Old Bailey on May 15, 2006. He was sentenced to a whole life tariff, meaning that he will never be released and will die behind bars. "You are a dangerous predator to women," the judge said in his summation. "This sentence will ensure you will never have the opportunity to prey on a young woman again."

For Rochelle's heartbroken parents it was a case of too little, too late. A monster had been allowed into their midst and had snatched away the most precious thing they possessed, the life of their beloved daughter.

Bad Rabbi

By most measures, Fred Neulander had led a successful life. Born into a middle class family in Queens, New York, in 1941, Fred had gone on to graduate from Trinity College in Hartford, Connecticut, with a degree in religious studies. He'd then accepted a position as assistant rabbi at Temple Emanuel in Cherry Hill, New Jersey, remaining there until 1974, when he founded his own congregation, M'Kor Shalom Reform Temple, also in Cherry Hill. Fred had married well, too. His college sweetheart, Carol, turned out to be an astute businesswoman, founding a specialist bakery, Classic Cakes, in 1990. When she sold the company for millions of dollars just four years later, she was asked to stay on and manage the business. By then, the couple's daughter, Rebecca, had left home, and their youngest son, Ben, was away at college. Older son, Matthew, was working as a paramedic and still lived at the couple's upscale Cherry Hill home.

On the evening of Tuesday, November 1, 1994, Fred and Matthew were at home enjoying a pizza before Matthew set off to start his 12-hour EMT shift. Carol was still at work, a typical situation on Tuesday evenings, which was when she held her weekly staff meetings. That left Fred home alone, but not for long. On this particular evening, he decided to sit in on a religious class at the temple. This was unusual, since Fred had not attended one of these seminars in over a year. Nonetheless, for a couple of hours, until Carol got home, the house stood empty.

Classes at the synagogue ended at around 8:50 that evening, and Fred then said goodbye to his congregants and pottered around in his office for a while before making the short journey home. He arrived at around 9:20 and noticed almost immediately that something was wrong. There, on the hardwood surface by the front door, were two dime-sized drops of blood. In fact, as Fred now realized, there was a trail of droplets leading into the interior of the house. Following that trail brought him to the tragic sight of his wife lying face down on the lounge floor, a patch of crimson matted in her hair. Fred did not even pause to check for a pulse. He immediately picked up the phone and dialed 911.

As the call went out to police and emergency responders in the area, one of the first to pick up on it was Matthew Neulander. Recognizing his own address, Matthew immediately told his driver to step on it. He arrived minutes later to find the police stringing up crime scene tape in front of his house. Matthew tried to enter the property but was prevented from doing so by a couple of burly patrolmen. He knew instinctively that that could only mean one thing. Whoever was inside was beyond medical help. But who was it? His mother? His father? That answer was provided to him when he spotted Fred sitting on a bench beside the garage, staring blindly into space, seemingly oblivious to the frigid night air. Matthew rushed over to his father but found Fred unresponsive to his questions. As he walked away crying, Fred did not even try to comfort him.

By now, the Cherry Hill police had been able to determine a few things about the murder. Carol had been killed by blunt force trauma with the killer apparently carrying the murder weapon from the scene. There was no sign of forced entry, meaning that Carol had either let her attacker in willingly or had been ambushed as she entered the house. But what was the motive? There was no indication that the place had been robbed, no sign of sexual assault. Why then had the 52-year-old businesswoman been killed? Fred had a possible answer. He said that he had warned his wife several times about bringing home cash from the bakery. She always carried the day's take in her burgundy purse, he said. A search of the house failed to turn up the purse in question.

Fred had a different story to tell when he phoned his daughter, Rebecca. He told her only that her mother had "met with an accident" and suggested that she drive over. Rebecca arrived some twenty minutes later to find a sizeable crowd, mainly from Fred's congregation, gathered outside the house. As she learned the dreadful truth and huddled for comfort with her brother Matthew, Rebecca was shocked by her father's demeanor. He'd just lost his wife of 29 years to a violent crime and yet he appeared not to have a care in the world.

At around 1 a.m. that morning, Fred, Rebecca and Matthew were taken to the Cherry Hill police station to make their respective statements. Matthew was interviewed first, then Rebecca, which meant that it was 3:20 a.m. before Fred eventually got to talk to detectives. Fred appeared calm and composed as he told the officers that he knew of no one who might want to harm his wife. He also assured the officers that there were no problems in their marriage and that there was definitely no infidelity – by either party.

But that conflicted with what Matthew had told the police earlier. According to him, relations between his parents were strained. Just two days before the murder, they had been involved in a furious argument when Carol had asked Fred whether they could work things out and Fred had told her, "It's over." Carol had then fetched some suitcases from a closet and had thrown them at Fred, screaming at him, "Get out!" She'd then told Matthew to "say goodbye to your father because he's leaving."

Rebecca had shared what was potentially an even more important piece of information. She'd told the police about an incident that had happened on the night of October 25, one week before the murder. On that occasion, Rebecca had called her mother on her car phone while she was driving home from her Tuesday night staff meeting. The conversation had continued after Carol pulled into her driveway. Carol told her daughter that there was a man tapping on the window. She then spoke to the man with Rebecca still on the line. Rebecca heard him say that he was delivering something for Fred. Carol then ended the call with her daughter but later told her about the strange incident involving this individual, who she dubbed "Bathroom Man."

According to Rebecca, her mother had invited the man into the house to wait for Fred. The man had then asked if he could use the bathroom. When he emerged a few minutes later, he told Carol that he couldn't wait. After placing something on the counter he left. When Carol checked the item, it turned out to be an empty envelope. Was this the item he'd been meant to deliver?

On the night of the murder, Carol had again been talking to Rebecca when she broke off the call to answer a knock at the door. She'd then looked through the peephole and informed her daughter that it was "Bathroom Man." Rebecca then heard her open the door and invite the man in out of the cold. She heard another voice, too, indicating that there was someone else with Bathroom Man. Rebecca was concerned about her mother letting two strangers into the house. She offered to stay on the line with her mother until her father got home, but Carol said that it wasn't necessary. They ended the call soon after.

Given the proximity of this encounter to the murders, this was a vital piece of information. However, when detectives asked Fred about it, he denied that he'd asked anyone to make a delivery to his house. He admitted that Carol had told him about her earlier encounter with Bathroom Man but said that he did not know who the man was. But this didn't make sense to the police. If Fred had told his wife that he did not know the delivery man, how likely was it that she would have allowed him into her house a second time? From that moment, Fred Neulander was elevated to the upper reaches of the suspect list.

And Fred's subsequent behavior did little to discourage the notion that he was somehow involved in his wife's death. As he and his children began to observe Shiva, the traditional Jewish period of mourning, Fred seemed decidedly upbeat. He even cracked jokes with mourners and assured them that the police would never catch Carol's killer. When a close family friend suggested that they elicit donations to hire a private detective, Fred said that any money collected should be given to him.

By now, there were also rumors circulating about the good rabbi. It appeared that he was quite the ladies' man, with a string of affairs to his name. One persistent story was that he was currently involved with Philadelphia radio host, Elaine Soncini. This was given credence when police checked Fred's phone records and found that he made multiple calls per day to Soncini's number, including on the day after Carol's murder. Then officers staked out Soncini's home and saw the rabbi arrive and pull his car into the garage as though he owned the place.

On December 5, investigators pulled Elaine Soncini in for questioning and asked her about the affair, a potential motive in the death of Carol Neulander. But Soncini was adamant that there was nothing untoward in her relationship with Fred. According to her, she had met the rabbi two years earlier when her husband was dying of cancer and he had provided her with grief counseling. There was nothing more to it than that.

But by the following morning, Soncini had decided to come clean. She phoned the police and admitted that she and Fred Neulander were lovers and had been since a week after her husband's death. According to Soncini, they met every day for sex, sometimes at her home, sometimes in Fred's office at the synagogue. Three months into the relationship, Fred had told her that he planned on divorcing Carol to be with her. When he failed to follow through on that promise, Elaine had given him an ultimatum. Unless he finalized things by January 1, 1995, she would end the affair.

Fred went one better than that. He told her that they would be together by her next birthday, December 17, 1994. According to Fred, he'd had a premonition that Carol would meet a violent end. That "premonition" would, of course, be realized. However, when Fred proposed to Elaine immediately after his seven-day period of mourning was concluded, she turned him down and asked him never to call her again. His cavalier attitude towards his wife's violent end had given her pause for thought.

In January 1995, the police persuaded Elaine Soncini to call Fred and try to get him to make an admission of murder while they listened in. Fred, however, was far too savvy for that. Despite Soncini's none-too-gentle probing, he steadfastly denied involvement in Carol's death, instead blaming the "Colombians who worked at the bakery."

It was a disappointing setback, but at least the police were making progress in other areas of the investigation. They had learned, for example, that Elaine Soncini was not Fred's only mistress. They'd also found out about an unusual connection between Fred and a low-life private investigator named Len Jenoff. Fred had recently engaged Jenoff to look into his wife's murder, which seemed a strange arrangement since Jenoff was an alcoholic who no one would hire on account of his unreliability. Was this a ruse intended to fake concern? Had Neulander picked Jenoff because he was the one individual who had virtually zero chance of uncovering anything incriminating? The police didn't know, but it did look suspicious.

During the first half of 1998, Camden County prosecutors began an in-depth review of the evidence in the Neulander case. It was far from conclusive. Fred Neulander had motive and opportunity; he had an alibi which seemed remarkably fortuitous; he had made utterances against his wife; he had lied to the police. However, there was no direct evidence linking him to the crime. Bringing Neulander before a jury would, therefore, be a huge risk. If he were to be acquitted, the double jeopardy rule would apply, meaning that he could never be tried for Carol's murder again.

The D.A., nonetheless, decided to go for it. On September 10, 1998, officers arrived at Fred Neulander's place of work and took him into custody. At the subsequent arraignment, he entered a not guilty plea and was released on $400,000 bail. Trial was set for June 2000 with Neulander's attorneys declaring themselves confident of an acquittal and a complete restoration of their client's reputation.

Unfortunately for them, the case was about to take a massive turn in the prosecution's favor. In late April 2000, Camden County prosecutor, Lee Solomon, got an unexpected call from a woman named Nancy Phillips, a reporter with the Philadelphia Inquirer. Philips said that she had information on the Neulander case and wanted to meet. That meeting took place at a diner in Audubon, New Jersey, on April 28, but Philips did not come alone. She brought Len Jenoff, Fred Neulander's hapless P.I., with her.

Jenoff cut straight to the chase. He had been involved in the murder of Carol Neulander and had acted under instructions from her husband. According to Jenoff, the rabbi had approached him in the Spring of 1994 asking for his assistance in an unusual matter. Neulander had told him that there was "an enemy of the state of Israel" living in Cherry Hill, New Jersey, a woman who he would pay $30,000 to have eliminated. Because Jenoff felt that he owed the rabbi, he agreed to go along with it.

Neulander had then laid out his plan. He wanted the murder to look like a botched robbery. He told Jenoff that he would get him into the woman's home by telling her to expect a delivery. Jenoff was then to enter the house, bludgeon the woman to death and steal a burgundy clutch bag, which Neulander assured him would be there. He could keep whatever money was in the bag (which Neulander said would be substantial) in addition to his $30,000 fee. Jenoff swore now that he did not know that the target was actually Fred Neulander's wife. He only found out, he claimed, when he read about it in the papers.

The date for the murder was scheduled for Tuesday, October 25. But Jenoff had panicked once he was inside the woman's house, had asked to use the bathroom and had left immediately after. The following day, Neulander was furious at his failure to follow through. He'd already paid Jenoff a deposit of $7,500 and now wanted results. He reset the date for the following Tuesday, November 2, and warned Jenoff not to slip up this time.

But still Jenoff wasn't sure whether he could actually bludgeon a complete stranger to death. He therefore recruited help, in the form of 21-year-old Paul Michael Daniels, his roommate at the halfway house where he was staying. Daniels, a drug addict, was all in once he heard of the money involved.

On the night of the murder, Jenoff and Daniels knocked on the door of the Neulander residence. Carol was on the phone when they arrived, but she recognized Jenoff and gestured them inside. The two men waited until she had concluded her call before they struck. According to Jenoff, it was Daniels who beat Carol Neulander to death, using a metal pipe that they had brought with them. (Daniels would later dispute this, saying that Jennoff struck the first blow and that he struck Carol twice more as she lay on the floor).

Either way, it was bad news for Fred Neulander. With both Jenoff and Daniels striking deals in exchange for their testimony, he never stood a chance. Still, it would take two trials to convict him. The first, in November 2001, was declared a mistrial, after the jury became deadlocked. The second, in October 2002, delivered guilty verdicts for capital murder, felony murder, and conspiracy.

While his co-accused were convicted of aggravated manslaughter and each got 23 years in prison with parole in ten, Fred Neulander was sentenced to life behind bars. Parole was not ruled out in his case, but the rabbi will be a very old man indeed by the time he becomes eligible.

I Love You to Death

Michelle Mills

Eddie Miller was the quintessential "Gentle Giant." The gregarious 6-footer had an outgoing nature and a devilish sense of humor that had gained him a large circle of friends. He had a close and loving relationship with his mum, Sara. On the work front, the 18-year-old had just begun work as a barman at a hotel in Leicestershire, England, and his employer had almost immediately recognized his potential. Just weeks into his new job, Eddie had been registered for a hotel management course at a local college. It seemed that life could not get any better. But then it did.

Michelle Mills was eleven years older than Eddie with two children from previous relationships. She was petite and pretty, a four-foot-eleven blonde bombshell with the kind of bubbly, fun-loving personality that was irresistible to the naive Eddie. He could hardly keep his eyes off her the first time they met. He was deeply flattered when the beautiful older woman reciprocated his interest. Within a short time, they were an item, and Eddie was in love for the first time in his life.

But there were things that Eddie did not know about his new girlfriend. He didn't know, for example, that Michelle had mental health issues, that she was prone to depression and histrionic disorder. He didn't know that she exacerbated these problems by abusing drugs and alcohol. He didn't know that her erratic behavior had resulted in her children being taken into care. He also did not know that Michelle was a chronically promiscuous woman who, by her own admission, had slept with 70 men. And he did not know that she was violent, although many of her former lovers could have filled him in on the details. The diminutive Michelle was quick to use her fists and nails when someone annoyed her. And when that failed, she was known to reach for a kitchen knife.

Might Eddie have acted differently had he known these things from the start? Perhaps. Then again, perhaps not. It was clear to all who knew him that the young man was besotted. He also appeared to regard himself as Michelle's protector, the white knight who was going to rescue her from her troubled past.

Eddie's friends were less certain about his choice of partner. It is safe to say that Michelle did not form the best of impressions, especially as she liked boasting about her experiences with drugs and about all the men she'd slept with. And then there were the scratches and bruises that Eddie now seemed to be sporting on a regular basis. He always had some or other excuse to offer but his friends quickly began to suspect that Michelle was behind the injuries. And they were right.

The relationship was still in its infancy when Eddie first ran afoul of one of Michelle's rages. It started with her accusing him of ignoring her and spending too much time with his friends. Then came tearful accusations of infidelity and then those crocodile tears gave way to rage as Michelle attacked. Eddie towered over his girlfriend and easily outweighed her, but he was not the kind of man to fight back. Instead he took the blows and the abuse and allowed Michelle's ire to blow itself out. They ended up having passionate make-up sex that night, but Michelle's point had been made. From then on, Eddie's friends saw less and less of him.

But it wasn't only Eddie's friends who Michelle appeared to have an issue with. Eddie was at this stage still living at home with his mother, and Michelle seemed to resent the close bond they shared. This became another source of conflict, and although Michelle failed in her attempts to drive a wedge between them, Sara did begin to see less of her son. Often he'd go out in the evening saying that he would be spending the night at Michelle's house only to return in the early morning hours when Michelle threw him out. On those occasions, Sara would notice scratches and bruises, and Eddie would tell her that Michelle had "gone berserk" while they were arguing. He wouldn't hear of ending the relationship, though. Michelle has had a hard life, he'd tell his mother, I want to be there to help her face her demons.

To Sara, there was only one solution. Eddie obviously loved Michelle, and if that was his choice, then Sara wanted to support him. In 2011, she invited Michelle to live with Eddie under her roof, an offer which Michelle gladly accepted. And, for a time, it seemed to go well. Sara became a friend and confidant to her son's girlfriend; she convinced Michelle to attend therapy and to take her anti-depressant pills; she implored her to cut down her alcohol intake and to give up drugs.

But with a woman as troubled as Michelle Mills, the truce was never going to last. One night, Sara heard shouting coming from her son's bedroom. Seeking to calm things down, she entered and saw Eddie pushed up against the wall taking no steps to protect himself as Michelle attacked. Sara dragged her away, but Michelle kept coming back until eventually Sara was able to force her from the room and close the door behind her. Then Michelle walked into the bathroom and punched a mirror, smashing it.

After that incident, Sara asked Michelle to move out, although she later thought better of it and invited her back. She would remain there until the summer of 2012, when she and Eddie moved into a rented cottage in the nearby village of Scalford. Soon neighbors would have front row seats to the blazing rows between the hulking six-foot Eddie and his petite 4-ft-11 girlfriend. Notwithstanding the size differential, it was always obvious who was the aggressor. And it wasn't Eddie.

In late October 2012, a rumor began circulating that Michelle had cheated on Eddie by sleeping with one of her ex-boyfriends, a man who Eddie knew. Eddie was deeply hurt by the stories, and for a time, his friends hoped that he would finally break up with Michelle. But Michelle apparently managed to convince him that the stories were untrue and Eddie stayed. Then, on the evening of November 5, 2012, the couple were at a local pub when the argument flared again. This time, however, Eddie was not prepared to get into it and left, walking home alone. Michelle, meanwhile, remained at the pub where she continued drinking. After watching a fireworks display scheduled for 10 p.m., she too left, walking home somewhat the worse for drink. A short while after her arrival at 10:15, neighbors heard the familiar refrain of shouts and threats coming from next door. The racket would continue until after midnight when they finally fell silent. A half hour later, the neighbors were roused by another cacophony, the wail of approaching sirens.

The police were responding to a 999 call from a woman who had told them that she'd stabbed her boyfriend after he'd attacked her. They arrived expecting to find a domestic violence incident. What they found instead was a slaughter. Eddie Miller had been stabbed multiple times in what would later be described as a frenzied attack. Fitting the pieces together, crime scene technicians would determine that the first thrust had driven the knife into Eddie's back as he sat on the couch. He'd tried to defend himself, sustaining deep lacerations to his hands but failing to throw off his much smaller attacker. She had continued thrusting with the blade, a large kitchen knife until it eventually snapped off in her victim's chest. By then, Eddie Miller was lying unconscious on the floor having suffered 24 deep wounds.

And yet, Eddie's life might still have been saved had Michelle picked up the phone and called the emergency services immediately. She didn't. Instead she sat for twenty minutes, watching the man she professed to love bleeding to death on the floor. By the time the ambulance arrived, it was already too late. Eddie died on the way to the hospital.

Michelle, of course, tried to blame everything on Eddie. She told the police that she was a victim of domestic violence and that Eddie regularly beat her. On the night in question, she said that he had become enraged after she told him that she was still in love with her ex-boyfriend. He had grabbed her by the throat. She'd had no option but to defend herself.

Unfortunately for Michelle, the evidence said different. She was charged with murder and appeared at Lincoln Crown Court in April 2013 to answer those charges. There, a jury made short shrift of her version of events. Found guilty, she was sentenced to life in prison with a minimum of 15 years to be served before she becomes eligible for parole.

"I detect no remorse in you," the judge said in delivering his sentence. "You are only concerned with yourself." That is as succinct a description of Michelle Mills's character as you are likely to find.

Motive Unknown

Thomas McFarland

Patrick Murray was exhausted after completing his late shift as a
subway conductor on the Brooklyn-Manhattan Transit line. It was 3:55
a.m. on the morning of April 1, 1935, and all Murray wanted was to
get off his feet and into bed. He wasn't at his most observant as he
entered the two-story dwelling where he lived on Marine Avenue,
Brooklyn. Nonetheless, he couldn't help but notice that the hall light
was on. This was unusual since his landlady, 68-year-old Nora Kelly,
was a stickler on matters of economy. She always turned out the lights
when she retired for the evening. Well, perhaps she forgot tonight,
Murray decided as he trudged up the stairs towards the apartment that
he shared with his wife and four-year-old daughter. He was too tired to
care.

But the next indicator that all was not well in the house was more
difficult to ignore. Mrs. Kelly had a dog, a lovable Collie mix named
Brownie. Usually, Brownie spent her days tied up in the back yard, but
at night Mrs. Kelly always bedded her down in the building's
basement. Although not today apparently. Brownie was still chained

up outside, and her mournful howls were pitiful. Within minutes of getting into bed, Murray had to get up again. He knew that he would get no peace while the dog kept up her ruckus, and so he went downstairs to check on her.

The dog's howls subsided to a whimper as Murray approached, but clearly she was agitated about something. Murray couldn't understand why Mrs. Kelly had neglected the animal so. She'd never done so in the past. Perhaps she'd gone to visit one of her daughters and had decided to stay overnight. Yes, that might explain the neglected dog, and the burning hall light, too. In any case, Murray had to take care of Brownie. At least he could put her in the cellar where he was sure she'd calm down.

Except that Brownie didn't calm down. The minute Murray released her chain, she made a dash to the cellar door and started pawing at it. "Take it easy, girl," Murray said soothingly. He then swung open the door at which Brownie immediately charged inside, heading for the darkness at the rear of the cellar, whining and yapping excitedly.

Murray might just have left her there. He was certainly tired enough to head upstairs and fall back into bed. But something told him that all was not right here. And so he played his flashlight across the darkened space that the dog had retreated to. That was when he saw her, his landlady Mrs. Kelly, hanging by her neck from a rope attached to the rafter. No, not a rope, he now realized. It was a length of insulated telephone wire. Backing out, leaving Brownie to whine over her dead mistress, Murray turned and ran. He did not stop until he reached the all-night diner at the corner of Fourth Avenue. It was from there that he called the police.

Detectives Edward Swift and Fred Kuhne, of the NYPD's 64th
Precinct, were the officers who responded to the call. They found
Murray waiting for them in front of the house and were directed by
him down to the basement where Brownie stood protectively in front
of her mistress's dangling body. It took all of Pat Murray's strength to
pull the dog away. Only then could the detectives get closer to
examine the body.

Initially, the consensus was that Mrs. Kelly had committed suicide.
Murray was asked about this and admitted that he could not think of a
single reason why his landlady might want to kill herself. Mrs. Murray
was in good health for her age. She had financial problems, sure, but
those had been with her for most of her life and were unlikely to
suddenly drive her to suicide. Besides, she had a very close
relationship with her 18-year-old niece Florence McVey.

"The girl lives here?" one of the detectives asked.

"No," Murray replied. "But she visits every day and sometimes stays
over."

The detective nodded and wrote something down in his book. Just
then, his partner called out to him. "Hey, Ed, come and take a look at
this."

Flashlights swept across the basement as Ed Swift crossed the space to where his partner was standing. What Detective Kuhne wanted to point out was drag marks etched in the furnace dust on the floor.

"Interesting," Swift said. "You think she was dragged here?"

"Nah," Kuhne responded. "Probably sweep marks left by her skirts." He then proceeded to cut the old lady's body down, and he and Swift gently lowered her to the ground. This wouldn't happen at a modern crime scene, of course, at least not until the CSIs had gone over it with a fine-toothed comb. But forensic detection was less evolved back then and, in any case, was trumped by decorum. Having done the decent thing, the detectives headed upstairs.

Mrs. Kelly's apartment consisted of a front parlor, dining room, kitchen, two bedrooms and a bathroom. The detectives entered via the kitchen where Mrs. Kelly's evening meal of meat balls and onions still sat untouched on the table, alongside a half-finished glass of milk and two coffee cups. Nothing appeared to have been disturbed, and it was the same story in the dining room. Everything seemed to be in its place. The officers then entered the front parlor, and it was there that they found Florence McVey, stretched out on the sofa. She was fully clothed, lying on her back with her head tilted to one side. One might almost have assumed that she was sleeping until one of the officers checked for a pulse and found none.

A cursory examination showed that there were no obvious injuries to the body – no cuts or bruises, no sign of bleeding. This led the detectives to believe that there might be a natural explanation for the double tragedy. Perhaps Florence McVey had suffered a sudden heart attack and died (this is unusual but not unheard of in the young); perhaps her grandmother had found her and been so distressed that she'd gone down to the cellar and hanged herself. Or perhaps, Florence had arrived and found her grandmother hanging in the cellar and the stress of it all had induced cardiac failure. In the absence of injuries on the bodies and any signs of a struggle within the apartment, both scenarios seemed viable.

But they were also premature. Before any conclusions could be drawn, the bodies needed to be examined by the medical examiner, and for that they had to be removed to the Kings County Morgue. While the investigators were waiting for the results of those autopsies, they did some more checking and uncovered a detail that might lend validity to their theory. Florence McVey had recently been unwell. In fact, she'd left work early on the day she died, complaining of a sore throat and headache. Had that been an early indicator of the condition that would cause her death just hours later? Again, it was possible but not yet proven. Not until the M.E.'s report was in.

And that report would not be long in coming. Within eight hours of the discovery of the bodies, deputy medical examiner Dr. Emanuel Marten called the office of District Attorney William Geoghan. What he had to say would blow the detectives' neat theory out of the water. Florence McVey had been raped and had most likely died of suffocation. Mrs. Kelly had also been sexually assaulted and had suffered crushing injuries to her chest. She'd more than likely already been dead by the time her killer strung her up in the basement.

But who would have done such a thing to a harmless old lady and an innocent 18-year-old? The detectives started where they always start such investigations – with the family of the dead women. Mrs. Kelly's relatives were quickly rounded up and brought down to the station for questioning, with assistant district attorney Vincent Ferreri and police Captain Frank Bals leading the interrogations.

Those interrogations, however, produced no leads. The police learned that Florence McVey had been raised by her grandmother after her father abandoned the family and her mother remarried. They learned also that Mrs. Kelly had three other daughters, one of whom had died. She also had a son, Edward Kelly, who was unemployed and homeless and, unlike the other children, was estranged from his mother. For a time, Edward was the chief suspect, but when he was cleared by an alibi, the investigation was back to square one.

Here's what the police had so far. Two women had been raped and killed by someone who they had apparently allowed into their apartment. There were no signs of a struggle and no one, not even Mrs. Eleanor Murray living upstairs, had heard anything. It all pointed to a killer who was known to the victims, and yet everyone who fit into that category had been cleared. Well, all except one, a suspect who the police were soon to learn about.

On April 2, a woman showed up at the headquarters of the Tenth Inspection District and said that she might have information pertinent to the Kelly-McVey murders. Ushered in to see Captain Bals, the woman introduced herself as Mrs. Eleanor Meyers and said that she was a friend of Nora Kelly. She then launched into a quite extraordinary story.

According to Mrs. Myers, she'd gone to visit her friend at around nine o'clock the previous evening. She'd rung the doorbell several times but had gotten no response. Finally, deciding that Mrs. Kelly wasn't home, she'd turned to leave. It was at that moment that the door swung open and a young man peered out. Mrs. Myers recognized him. He was Nora Kelly's son-in-law, Tom McFarland, the husband of her deceased daughter, Anne.

"What did he say when he opened the door?" Captain Bals wanted to know.

"That Mrs. Kelly wasn't home," Mrs. Myers replied. "I then asked him to let her know that I had called and then I left. I didn't think anything of it until I heard of poor Nora's death."

This was a very valuable lead and one that the police wasted no time in following up. They learned that McFarland was a native of Mobile, Alabama, and that he'd met Mrs. Kelly's daughter while serving in the army at Fort Hancock. They had married that same year and had their first child, Marian, a year later in 1921. Three years after that, Anne McFarland had been pregnant with twins but had died in childbirth. Thereafter, Thomas and the three children had moved in with Nora Kelly and had remained under her roof until November 1934, when Thomas had moved them to a new home on Humboldt Street, Brooklyn.

Thomas McFarland thus had a lot to thank his mother-in-law for. Was it possible that after she'd shown him such kindness, McFarland had raped and killed her, then hung her up in the basement like a carcass? There was only one way to find out, and McFarland was therefore picked up from his place of work on Long Island and brought in for questioning.

Initially, McFarland denied the murders of Florence and Mrs. Kelly. However, the persistence of the interrogators eventually wore him down, and after five hours of intense questioning, he finally cracked and agreed to tell them what had happened.

He said that he'd left home at around two o'clock Sunday afternoon to visit his mother-in-law. On the way to her house, he'd stopped at a bar where he'd consumed five glasses of beer. He'd also bought a bottle of sherry before continuing on, arriving in the early evening. Mrs. Kelly let him into the apartment, and Florence was also there, lying down on the couch because she was not feeling well. McFarland had opened the bottle of sherry and offered his mother-in-law a drink, which she had refused. He'd then had a drink himself and consumed several more before Mrs. Kelly told him to stop. "She said I was making a pig of myself," McFarland told the officers. Then she asked him to leave, even (according to McFarland) picking up a kitchen chair and threatening him with it.

That's when everything went black and I think I choked her," McFarland said. Florence, attracted by the ruckus, then entered the kitchen. She demanded to know what he had done and in response McFarland grabbed her by the throat and strangled her. According to him, he was afraid that she might go for a knife that was on the sideboard.

Asked about the sexual assaults on the two women, McFarland claimed that he did not remember doing anything like that. His claim that "everything went blank" was something that the investigators had heard before. It is a common defense used by killers who are trying to avoid responsibility for their actions.

Thomas McFarland went on trial in January 1936. His defense tried to argue that he might have committed the murders while in a trance as he often experienced blackouts due to shell-shock suffered during the war. They even put his young daughter, Marian, on the stand to testify that her father was often "dizzy," got "excited over nothing," and sometimes lost track of time. At one point during her testimony, the child begged McFarland to look at her, bursting into tears when he continued to stare at the ground, a posture he maintained through most of the trial.

Marian's plaintive cries of "Daddy, please look at me!" even coaxed tears from some of the jury members, but it did not influence their decision. Thomas McFarland was found guilty of two counts of first-degree murder and sentenced to death. He died in the electric chair at Sing Sing on August 20, 1936. To this day, no one truly understands the motive behind his crimes.

For more True Crime books by Robert Keller

please visit:

http://bit.ly/kellerbooks